"Written by two master clinicians with decades of experience, this is a compassionate, science-based approach to responding effectively to anger. Many of the strategies we use to try to 'control' or avoid anger end up backfiring, further increasing pain and shame. Instead, this workbook offers practical tools that will help you understand anger and develop the skills needed to live in line with your values, even when anger is present."

—**Jenna LeJeune, PhD**, licensed clinical psychologist; president of Portland Psychotherapy Clinic, Research, and Training Center; peer-reviewed acceptance and commitment therapy (ACT) trainer; and coauthor of *Values in Therapy*

"This is not yet another hokey book on how to get rid of anger. Instead, we learn that anger is something we all experience. It is part of being human, not something to be ashamed of. Armed with this pivotal insight—and armed with their own personal histories of growing up around anger—the authors do a masterful job of taking us on a scientifically based, step-by-step exploration of the inner workings of our anger, and how we can both welcome it and manage it to our lasting benefit. If you have ever felt your anger is over the top, or felt helpless to do anything about it, this is the book for you. Highly recommended."

—**Kirk Strosahl, PhD**, cofounder of ACT, and coauthor of *The Mindfulness and Acceptance Workbook for Depression*

"Two of our most tender voices in ACT, Robyn and Manuela, have created a guide to show us the way from 'anger is bad' to 'anger is interesting'. Brief, and packed with powerful exercises, this book is a must for both suppressors and those who act out. Read it and learn to be sweet to yourself (and your vulnerability) as you do what matters."

—**Patricia Robinson, PhD**, director of training at Mountainview Consulting, director of innovation at Interprofessional Primary Care Institute of Oregon, and coauthor of *The Mindfulness and Acceptance Workbook for Depression* and *The Depression Toolkit*

"In this clear, engaging, and deeply useful book, Walser and O'Connell have created a truly unique offering. *The ACT Workbook for Anger* masterfully guides us to a compassionate understanding of why we struggle with anger, and offers powerful tools to help those who struggle with this challenging emotion—not by trying to control our anger or shaming ourselves for having it, but by deeply engaging with what is most important to us. A vital resource for all who struggle with anger, and for those who seek to help them. Highly recommended!"

—**Russell Kolts, PhD**, professor of psychology at Eastern Washington University, and author of *The Compassionate Mind Guide to Managing Your Anger* and *CFT Made Simple*

"Superficially, anger is something that *must* be controlled, but that only applies to angry behavior. Anger the emotion can be a wise companion, helping you to see your own fears and vulnerabilities from a place of genuine self-compassion. That is what this well-written and wise book will teach you how to do. If you've caused terrible pain for yourself or those you love by acting out of anger, freezing in place in the face of anger, losing your boundaries, or hiding from yourself to suppress anger, it's time to learn how to relate to this basic human emotion in a new way. Pick up this book and begin."

—**Steven C. Hayes, PhD**, Nevada Foundation Professor in the department of psychology at the University of Nevada, Reno; and originator and codeveloper of ACT

"Repeated anger behavior can damage our lives, our families' lives, and even our larger community/culture. *The ACT Workbook for Anger* offers transformative processes to change anger-driven behavior into values-based actions, to accept angry feelings and thoughts without turning them into attacks, and to replace anger judgements with compassion and forgiveness. Highly recommended."

—**Matthew McKay, PhD**, coauthor of *ACT on Life Not on Anger* and *When Anger Hurts*

The
ACT
WORKBOOK for
ANGER

**MANAGE EMOTIONS & TAKE BACK YOUR LIFE
WITH ACCEPTANCE & COMMITMENT THERAPY**

**ROBYN D. WALSER, PhD
MANUELA O'CONNELL**

New Harbinger Publications, Inc.

Distributed in Canada by Raincoast Books

NEW HARBINGER PUBLICATIONS is a registered trademark of New Harbinger Publications, Inc.

Copyright © 2021 by Robyn D. Walser and Manuela O'Connell
        New Harbinger Publications, Inc.
        5674 Shattuck Avenue
        Oakland, CA 94609
        www.newharbinger.com

Printed with permission from Many Rivers Press, www.davidwhyte.com. Author, title of poem, title of source book shall be listed, together with ©Many Rivers Press, Langley, WA USA.

Cover design by Amy Daniel

Acquired by Ryan Buresh

Edited by Kristi Hein

All Rights Reserved

Library of Congress Cataloging-in-Publication Data on file

Printed in the United States of America

23   22   21

10   9   8   7   6   5   4   3   2   1   First Printing

I would like to dedicate this book to my mother, Susan L. Pickett,
a woman who suffered at the hands of anger, survived, and thrived.

—RDW

For all who have a vulnerable part that longs to be heard, seen, and loved,
may you each receive these experiences and be free to live fully.

—MO

Contents

Acknowledgments

I would like to thank all those women in my life who have recognized the power and importance of emotion. Supporting me in feelings of love, sadness, joy, anxiety…and yes, even anger.

—RDW

First, I want to acknowledge my mentor and dear friend Robyn Walser for the amazing experience of writing this book together. Her presence, in each of its forms, is such a gift in my life! Always a wise, fullhearted, learning adventure…grateful beyond words.

I owe an enormous debt of gratitude to the Association for Contextual Behavioral Science (ACBS) community for being a family wherein every voice has a place and is a nurturing context for growth.

A deep bow to all of the human beings I have had the privilege to help in one way or another, both clients and students. Our intimate connections help us recognize the complexity of being human, and remind us to trust that we are on this journey of awakening together.

Finally, to my family, Daniel, Demian, and Alejo, thank you for all of the daily support you give; you are the other side of my dedication to helping the world.

—MO

Introduction

Anybody can become angry—that is easy, but to be angry with the right person and to the right degree and at the right time and for the right purpose, and in the right way—that is not within everybody's power, that is not easy.

—Aristotle

As a young child, I (RDW) witnessed the power and impact of anger. To whomever in my family the anger was directed, it was paramount to move quickly and do whatever was possible to stop the fury that was about to be unleashed. Frantic, panicked children dashed to clean, hide, be quiet, get small, or try to disappear so as to not be a victim of the impending rage. I learned that anger was dangerous and to be avoided. Growing up in a family where domestic violence was part of my experience, I came to understand how anger could work to control those around you and instill fear in all who experienced the tirade of the moment. This led me to fear my own as well as others' anger. Anger was a tool to control people, and I came to distrust those who expressed anger in inappropriate ways.

I (MO) grew up in a strict family; if anger was expressed, it was harshly punished. The severe and inflexible responses to emotion were tangible—and particularly harsh if the emotions were "not appropriate for a woman." I responded to this suppression of anger by overly regulating my own emotions. Anger was so well controlled throughout my life that it never visited me much at all. I became the "good girl." I collapsed my boundaries and stifled my authentic voice. This made me vulnerable to abuse situations. I also tended to regulate my behavior so I would not make other people angry, especially the ones I cared most about. This diminished my freedom. Although I didn't feel anger, oddly enough, I was a slave to avoiding it.

Our personal histories of learning about anger are part of what has drawn us to write this book. Both of us have encountered painful pasts linked to the emotional experience of anger. We have either been afraid of it or avoided it. This doesn't mean that we have not felt it. Anger is felt by all. However, what any of us learn in responding to anger likely dictates how we behave when we experience this emotion. Each of us has learned how we ought to react when we feel anger. The trouble is that sometimes these reactions are quite unhealthy, leaving us in pain, unable to respond or express anger appropriately.

Because you have picked up this book, we assume that you have struggled with anger in some important way. Your personal struggle with anger, whether it be suppressing it or acting on it in ways that lead to harm, is worth exploring, understanding, and changing, especially if you find yourself suffering "at the hands" of anger. If this suffering has left you feeling guilty, ashamed, powerless, and out of control, or if it has led to significant difficulties in your life related to loss of relationships, jobs, friendships and romance, and sense of self, then it is well worth your while to discover a new way to view anger and its role and place in your life.

The contents of this workbook will help you come to understand your own experiences of anger and how it impacts you as well as how you relate to your personal experience of it. Learning to recognize the roles that anger plays—both useful and harmful—will help you begin to discriminate how best to relate to your feelings of anger. It will also help you learn how to respond so that your needs are met, your goals attained, and your values lived.

Anger

Anger is an important emotion when expressed wisely. For instance, it can carry an important message needing your attention, such as when your personal boundaries are crossed. Recognizing this violation and responding to it in a particular way can help you recover when a relationship is in the balance. It can tell you that something is wrong and needs addressing. However, your reaction and relationship to anger will be the difference between a healthy and wise response to anger and one that is harmful to you and others.

Your relationship with feelings of anger is of significant consequence. It can mean the difference between relationships that are full and authentic and relationships filled with fear and control. How we relate to our anger and how we behave when we experience anger will bring us either a universe of freedom or a universe of control. Relating to anger unwisely or inflexibly interferes with living a rich and meaningful life. The lasting impact of anger for both the person expressing it and the person receiving that expression is substantial and worthy of your attention. Let's take a closer look.

Anger and Control

When we express anger in a dominant way, it can be viewed as an attempt to control others. Importantly, however, this is not just about controlling someone else—getting them to stop doing something they are doing or start doing something they have not been doing—it is also about avoiding a personal internal experience. That is, anger expressed in dominant ways is often secondary or in response to feeling other emotions, such as insecurity, fear, sadness, and anxiety. When we do not want to feel these emotions—perhaps because we don't like them or we see them as bad or weak—we may try to control them by becoming angry instead.

These types of control and avoidance are relatively universal. Most of us have learned to avoid emotions that are considered negative or unwanted. However, this kind of avoidance and control can govern our lives in such a way that it creates other problems. Those of you who are quick to anger or use anger to dominate and control others often pay a price—not just in others fearing you or disliking you, but also in the impact your anger has on you.

Letting Go of Control in the Service of Living Well

One goal of this book is to show you the cost of reacting to anger in impulsive, avoidant, and unwise ways. Note, however, that no emotion is problematic in and of itself. The issue is how we relate to emotions. So we won't line up with the notion that anger is a *bad* emotion. Indeed, we can learn to be present to anger and react to it in healthy ways. And we want to reassure you that not all anger is problematic. Sometimes anger is the exact experience that is called for; it may even motivate people to take healthy action.

Rather than changing the emotion, then, we'll work specifically on how to relate to anger in ways that assist with healthy boundaries, that feed relationships rather than destroy them, and that welcome anger in each of its healthy behavioral forms. Rather than seeing anger as an obstacle to healthy living, to be suppressed or expressed in ways that limit vitality, we'll focus on wise and flexible ways of relating to anger. Learning *to be with* anger and not a *puppet to* anger will be our goal.

Therefore, in your work with this book, you will learn to relate to your anger in new ways. We'll explore the contexts in which anger occurs and the different ways anger is expressed. You will work through problematic behavior related to anger, considering the underlying emotions that may be involved and learning how to instead meet these, openly and willingly. Learning how to let go will be part of this endeavor.

Onward

As noted, because you have picked up this book, it's likely that you or someone you know is struggling with anger or issues related to anger. Or you may recognize that anger is a part of life and simply want to find the best way to relate to it.

We ask the following questions to help you consider whether this book might be particularly relevant for you:

- Have you ever said or done something out of anger that caused terrible pain for the people you love the most?

- Have you experienced serious consequences in places or relationships that you care about while being hijacked by anger?

- Have you silently stayed in an abusive situation because anger wasn't allowed?

- Have you lost your boundaries in relation to others, giving up far more than you would like in order to keep the peace?

- Do you hide your anger or not tell others that you feel angry?

If you answered yes to any of these questions, this is the right book for you. Acknowledging this doesn't mean that there is something wrong with you. Nor does it mean that anger is your enemy. We'll meet you where you are, because we know that you're doing your best with what you know. Reactions to anger are often learned, developing out of what has been modeled for us or what we have been told about anger. We know that you didn't choose or intend for your angry reactions to be as they were—or continue to be.

We invite you to walk with us on a journey of acceptance—not of your anger-filled actions, but of your authentic self, with your genuine fears, pains, and vulnerabilities each allowed. We do so without leaving you alone or judging you. The goal is to help you build a wise and flexible relationship with anger in the service of a values-based life. Passing judgment will only make this process more difficult or unlikely. At times it may feel that things are messy, perhaps anxiety-producing—letting go of internal control means showing up to the very emotions you have been avoiding through anger. Not an easy job. However, if you hang in there, you may find that your relationship with anger transforms, becoming an informative companion rather than a bad experience.

Let's explore some additional questions to help you on your way while working with the material in this book. Your answers can be useful as you move forward, especially when feeling stuck while working with your own anger. Keeping your answers to these questions in mind might help if at any point you feel overwhelmed or worried that you might have a failure experience when trying to change your behavior.

If anger could be a wise companion:

- What would you start doing or stop doing; what would you do more of, or do less of?

- How would you like to treat yourself, others, life, the world, differently?

- What goals would you pursue that you aren't pursuing now?

- What people, places, events, activities, and challenges would you like to engage differently?

- What would be different for you in ways that really matter?

What You Will Discover from Reading This Book

While we all come from different backgrounds and have different experiences and relationships with anger, we assume that you will engage with this workbook with the intention to learn new behaviors. Dealing with anger isn't easy. It can feel vulnerable to talk about personal experiences of anger. This is part of why we went first: starting this introduction with our own stories.

You will discover that anger is a natural part of the human experience. You will also see the full impact of anger and how it influences us, in both negative and positive ways. You will learn how anger creates problems and how it can be useful in motivating us for change and action. We'll explore everything from everyday flashes of anger at life's vexations to boiling long-term anger. Even if anger isn't a lasting or explosive problem for you, you may find this book helpful in working through those moments in your day-to-day routine that elicit anger, prompting you to act out or suffer silently. You will learn about the different types of anger, such as seething anger and explosive anger. This will help you know what type or types of anger you are working on.

First, you'll learn to understand anger and its function, become mindful of it, and connect to its impact. The ultimate goal is to make responsible choices about how you want to act in the world—not by eliminating anger, but by instead seeing it for what it really is.

Given that we are focusing on the relationship to anger, we present a new model for thinking about and working with it. One critical aspect of our approach to anger is to separate the urge or impulse, the thought, the feelings or emotions, and the sensations of anger from the behaviors or actions of anger.

We'll explore the subtle and different nuances of context that elicit or get you in contact with anger. We want to help you notice and come to know your many ways of experiencing anger when it shows up. Learning to respond to it skillfully so that it no longer controls your actions will be a significant part of the work. You'll learn to instead wisely choose the actions you'll take when feeling angry. By engaging in "choiceful" and values-based actions in the face of anger, you will "see" its potential power and capacity to push you around, but you will no longer be a slave to it, despite these possibilities. Indeed, part of the work will be about observing the rise and fall of anger, noticing its comings and goings, and acting according to values instead of avoidance. It may seem counterintuitive, but this will give you a lot more control in your life! You'll have more control over what you say and do when anger shows up. You'll have more freedom to respond rather than react.

Acceptance and Commitment Therapy for Treating Anger

To begin this journey, in chapter 1 we'll review anger and its impact. We want to help you discover the full picture of your anger, recognizing the thoughts, feelings, and sensations as well as the patterns and functions that accompany it. Beginning with chapter 2, we'll explore the context of anger, and you'll begin learning how to respond to your anger when it occurs and how to discriminate when acting on anger is useful and when it is not by looking at anger from a particular therapeutic lens: acceptance and commitment therapy or ACT (said like the word *act*). In the chapters that follow, we'll explore ACT in depth and see how it's used to address and treat problematic anger.

ACT, developed by Dr. Steven Hayes and his colleagues (see Hayes, Strosahl, & Wilson, 2012), is a behavioral therapy that uses both mindfulness and awareness skills along with values and committed action skills to assist people in becoming more flexible in the service of living meaningful and purposeful lives. Lives guided by what is important rather than by any particular emotion or thought—this is a large part of the work done in ACT. Given this, we'll work on how you can guide your life based on what you care about instead of being guided by anger, yours or someone else's.

ACT has six core processes that help individuals become more consciously aware of their internal experience, learning how to be present to it instead of trying to control or avoid it. Once you are more able to observe what is happening when you're angry, noticing what is happening in your body and around you, you will be better positioned to make values-guided choices rather than simply acting on what you feel, sense, and think. Here are the six core processes and the chapters in which they're covered:

- Willingness to Experience (chapter 4)

- Defusion (chapter 5, Recognizing Mind)

- Present Moment (in chapters throughout the book)

- Self-as-Context or Perspective Taking (chapter 6, Who Am I? Contacting a Larger Sense of Self)

- Values Clarification (chapter 7, What Truly Matters)

- Committed Action (chapter 8, ACTing on What Matters)

We focus on each of these processes in turn in separate chapters (except present moment, which is woven throughout the book), helping you learn new ways to understand and relate to the emotional experience of anger. Many of the exercises we'll invite you to do involve being aware of what is happening in the moment, and we'll ask you to visit your current experience routinely. Chapters 1, 2, and 3 introduce you to understanding anger, understanding change, and letting go of control, respectively. The ultimate goal is to learn how to be more psychologically and behaviorally flexible in the service of creating meaningful lives.

In addition to the chapters on anger and ACT processes, two important chapters relate to healing from the damage that may have been caused by past angry episodes: Compassion and Anger (chapter 9) and Forgiveness and Anger (chapter 10). We round the book out with a final chapter focusing on the journey forward: in chapter 11 we summarize how anger can be used in positive ways concerning social justice, and we encourage you to continue the work started here.

How This Book Is Structured

We begin each chapter with a story of anger told by real people in real situations. The idea here is to get you connected to the work you will be doing by hearing stories that might feel similar to your own. As well, we can refer to these to demonstrate concepts that we hope will be useful to you.

Second, we explore particular concepts or ideas related to ACT and focus on the six core processes just introduced. We'll connect these to anger, its precursors, and its aftermath. Here we focus on things that you can learn and understand about anger, reviewing the concepts in a way that we hope leaves you feeling empowered to make a change.

We think that the best way to learn new behavior is to engage in activities that allow you to practice. So we routinely weave exercises into the chapters, allowing you to explore the processes not just with your mind through reading but also through experience. We strongly encourage you to engage with these exercises to reap the most benefit from this book. The words alone will not suffice, especially if you're interested in genuine change. There may be times when you don't feel like doing a particular exercise; some will be challenging and may bring up painful emotional experiences. But please hang in there and give it a try. If you need to, you can return later to any particular exercise.

Not all the exercises will be a good fit for everyone. Give each a try and see which ones are the best fit for you. Our wish for you is maximum benefit—and engaging in the exercises is the best way to ensure this outcome.

At each chapter's end, a summary will briefly review what has been covered in the chapter and link the work to the next chapter, building the overall story of creating flexibility in your life.

Our Personal Hope for You

As noted earlier in this introduction, we have both been victims of unwise ways of relating to anger, and we have experienced our own anger. On the one hand, having been at the receiving end of anger, we hope to prevent the negative outcomes that can stem from anger expressed in violent and harmful ways. Part of the work of this book is preventing or repairing the destructive nature of anger that's based on the need to exercise power and control, the need to be right, or protect one's ego. On the other hand, having felt our own anger and acted in ways that have led to regret, we also hope to find solace in forgiveness, compassion, repair, and a return to values-based living. And finally, if you have been suppressing anger for a long time, we truly hope that you can become an ally with your emotion, clarifying your boundaries and building your own true life.

CHAPTER 1

Understanding Anger

I am heartened to find so much wit in you, that you'd give thought to consequences and choose your way with reason, not passion only.

—Deborah J. Lightfoot

Jerold had struggled from a young age to feel safe and in charge. He had been bullied at an early age and could not seem to find the best way to manage the emotions he experienced during these times. Jerold felt sadness and humiliation. When alone, he would fantasize about beating the bullies, striking back to stop their taunts. His resentment grew, and his feelings of being out of control haunted him. Over time he began to act on this anger. He struck back.

During his teenage years, Jerold found himself in many fistfights characterized by resentment and fury. Jerold began to embody anger. To others, he seemed angry most of the time. His demeanor was threatening, and those around him came to understand how short his fuse to anger could be. Jerold often responded to small and large confrontations alike with bursts of rage. He would punch walls, break things, and physically attack those who disagreed with him. Jerold spent time in jail and lost many friendships and romantic partners who could not tolerate his rage. His sadness and humiliation from childhood never got the chance to heal through kind and supportive connections, and Jerold continued to feel out of control, despite his efforts to gain control through violence.

Angela learned as a small child that anger was "not allowed." She grew up in a family with strict rules and an overbearing father. Angela's father often proclaimed that he was the only person in the family allowed to be angry. Any expression of anger by others was either actively discouraged or punished. Angela saw her father become quite inflamed, at times striking her or her mother and brother in a fit of rage. She began to understand anger as scary and powerful.

Despite this history, Angela still felt anger. She could detect her feelings of anger, noticing that they ranged from annoyance to irritation to fury. However, anyone interacting with Angela would never know she had these experiences. She had learned to hide these emotions, deeply suppressing them, never expressing them. To be angry was to be punished, so Angela was afraid to be angry and afraid to express herself. She quietly accepted situations that called for her anger, submitting to others instead of asserting her needs and showing her emotion. This behavior was costly to Angela. She was often taken advantage of and rarely stood up for her own needs.

Defining Anger

We can separate the experience of anger into four general components: (1) a strong *feeling* of displeasure accompanied by a range of (2) *physiological* experiences or sensations, (3) *thoughts*, and (4) *actions*. When someone is feeling angry and expressing it outwardly, they may have a mix of intense feelings of displeasure. They may experience redness in the face and tightness of the muscles, repetitive thoughts about the incident that made them angry, and actions such as slamming cupboards or throwing things. Another example of someone who suppresses anger might again include the intense feeling of displeasure, as well as a sinking feeling in their stomach, anxious thoughts about hiding or getting away, and an action of fleeing the scene.

Although we can name these categories of feelings, physiological experiences or sensations, thoughts, and actions, we recognize that when someone is quite angry, they may not be so easy to sort out in the moment. These experiences can seem to be all meshed together. For example, some people report that they "see red" when they feel mad—an experience that is both a physiological sensation and a thought. Some people, when they become angry, literally turn red and experience sensations of heat. They might also report that their vision is narrowed and they actually see the color red. They are both seeing and feeling red.

The actions of anger can seem like the feeling of anger itself. Throwing things, for instance, is often blamed on the feeling of anger—as if the anger caused someone to throw an object. So although we are separating the experience of anger into four general components—feelings of displeasure accompanied by sensations, thoughts, and actions—we recognize that anger can be complicated. We'll explore your experiences of anger in these general categories momentarily. But first, we want to also acknowledge that anger is on a continuum and that each of you has your own personal learning history concerning anger. Let's take a closer look.

The Opposite Poles of Anger

The two stories of anger at the beginning of this chapter represent the possible poles of the emotion: Jerold representing full reactivity at one end of the pole, and Angela representing complete suppression at the other. You may have recognized yourself or parts of yourself in one of these two stories. You may also have recognized someone you know. Alternatively, you may have identified with only small pieces of these stories. Any reaction is okay. We all have our own stories of anger, and there is a range of anger experiences between the two opposite poles of anger.

Anger, although often described as red, has many colors. Anger is multidimensional; we each have many ways of feeling and expressing anger. You might observe this with your own feelings of anger, sometimes hiding it and sometimes acting on it. Indeed, feelings and expressions of anger can be quite different and often depend on the situation in which they occur. For instance, even if you generally overreact when you're angry, you may be aware of times you were angry but did not overreact. Maybe the situation or context forced you to modulate your response (if the police were present, for instance). If you tend to underreact to anger, often suppressing it, you may still be aware of times when you had significant reactions. Perhaps you surprised yourself by getting caught up in the emotion and yelling or stomping around.

Recognizing your feelings of anger and its expressions, as well as what triggers it and in what contexts it plays out, is part of understanding this emotion and learning to live with it healthily.

Personal Learning and the Character of Anger

Anger is normal. We human beings are fully designed to experience anger, and each person feels it, reacts to it, and understands it in their own way. Everyone also has a learning history that shapes their anger response, playing a role in how they experience it, relate to it, and express it. Those who helped raise you are a part of this historical picture. What you have learned from parents, friends, and others in your social world impacts how you relate to anger today.

From the earlier stories in this chapter, you can get a sense of what we mean. Jerold learned that aggressively acting on anger served to make others afraid of him. This behavior seemed to help him, but ultimately it failed. He was trying to not feel vulnerable, but his acting-out behavior only reminded him of how vulnerable he actually felt, leading to a cycle of anger. Angela was given strict rules about anger: it was not allowed. She also learned the dangers of anger acted on poorly as she witnessed the destructive consequences. Her history taught her that anger is wrong or bad, even harmful. Exploring and understanding your personal history will be valuable in starting to understand what you have learned about anger from those around you, what they told you about anger, and how they behaved when angry.

Exercise 1.1: Your Learning History and Anger

1. In the space provided, write down any rules you learned as a child or adolescent about anger and how it should be expressed. For example, *anger is bad and should never be revealed* or *anger gets others to respond to you quickly.* These rules could have been explicit—stated out loud directly—or implied—parents who never showed any anger imply that anger is not good.

    _____

    _____

    _____

    _____

    _____

2. In the space provided, write down what you've learned about anger by watching how others behaved when expressing their anger. For example, *anger is powerful: if you act out, you get what you want.*

    _____

    _____

    _____

    _____

    _____

Understanding your history of anger will help you better understand the way you respond to anger today. We carry rules and ways of behaving with us for a lifetime—sometimes without even being aware of the rules. Beginning to look at your history and the problems that rigid rules and problematic behavior created concerning anger is a first step toward doing things differently. We'll have more to say about this later; for now, it can be helpful to acknowledge how you speak about anger. Review the words and ways of describing anger that follow. Note any words that you have used to talk about your own experience. You are invited to circle the word or words.

Words for Describing Anger

Annoyance	Irritation	Resentment
Wrath	Gall	Outrage
Rage	Antagonism	Offense
Madness	Exasperation	Incensed
Aggravation	Fury	Indignation
Vexation	Crossness	Peevishness

Write down any additional words that we may have missed:

_____

_____

Knowing how you talk about anger can be a cue for recognizing it and making a change. For instance, if you're aware that you're feeling *annoyed,* this might be a signal that it is time to take healthy action. Doing something different, early on, is an alternative to letting the annoyance grow and become problematic.

Now that you have briefly explored the continuum of anger and how your learning history influences how you express anger, let's turn to the three individual components of anger that contribute to the overall feelings of displeasure discussed earlier. We'll explore each in turn, inviting you to complete the exercises to better understand your physiological response or sensations, thoughts, and actions related to anger.

Physiological Experiences of Anger

Explaining the physiological experience or sensations of the body while angry is a challenge, especially if we get into the weeds of what is happening in the body. We might find ourselves discussing things like vasoconstriction (constriction of blood vessels), pulse-volume amplitude (a measure of blood volume changes), or left-ventricular contractibility (performance of the heart ventricle at a given pressure). Scientists have measured these physiological responses when investigating anger (see Stemmler, Aue, & Wacker, 2007, for an example of this kind of research) in efforts to better understand the somatovisceral response to anger. Rather than going down this technical road, we take a less formal approach.

> Somatovisceral: *Soma* refers to the muscles and skeletal system of the body, and *visceral* refers to the organ system. Thus *somatovisceral* refers to the interplay between the structural body and its organs.

When we're angry, several physiological responses generally occur: our muscles become tense, our heart rate accelerates and blood pressure increases, and we breathe more rapidly. Our attention becomes narrowed, typically focusing on the target of our anger. We also tend to react with facial expressions such as narrowing of the brow and frowning. Our faces can also turn red. As well, brain chemicals and hormones are released. These can create a state of arousal lasting from hours to days, which can lower our threshold for reexperiencing anger as the initial physiological response begins to wear off.

Exercise 1.2: Noticing Your Physiological Responses to Anger

In the space provided, list the top five physical reactions you are aware of when you feel *slightly* angry or just irritated; for instance, tension in your shoulders, neck, or head.

1. _____

2. _____

3. _____

4. _____

5. _____

Rate the level of anger you need to experience to be aware of these bodily reactions by circling a number on the spectrum:

1	2	3	4	5

Low levels   High levels

In the space provided, list the top five physical reactions you are aware of when you feel *very* angry; for instance, tension all over your body and feeling hot.

1. _____

2. _____

3. _____

4. _____

5. _____

Rate the level of anger you need to experience to be aware of these bodily reactions by circling a number:

1	2	3	4	5

Low levels   High levels

If you find it challenging to recognize your physiological responses to anger, make a note here.

_____

_____

_____

What are the physiological cues that you notice, if any, *before* you become angry? For instance, feeling on edge or narrowed brows.

_____

_____

_____

Noticing your common bodily sensations and experiences of anger is part of growing your understanding of your relationship to anger. If you can't recognize your physiological responses to anger, it is harder to make healthy responses and choices when anger arises. If you're unsure about your physiological responses, don't worry; we'll be providing information about how to be more aware of your body. Awareness of your body and its emotional states is part of living with anger healthily.

Thought Experiences of Anger

Thought experiences of anger tend to be easier to identify than some of the physiological responses. For instance, it's easier to recognize a thought like *This is really making me angry* than it is to detect a rise in blood pressure (there's a reason high blood pressure is called the silent killer). However, this doesn't mean that anger can't short-circuit our thinking when we are in a heightened state of arousal. Reasoning or thoughts about the impact on others can be thwarted, and we can seemingly become blind to our own actions.

Our thoughts can also leap to trying to escape (*This is too scary; I need to get out of here*) or merely making whatever is causing the anger to stop (*Please make it stop*). Sometimes our thoughts during anger seem more jumbled or chaotic. They can bounce around as we try to sort out what is happening and why we feel the way we do. Other times the anger feels so intense that we seem to have only one or two thoughts, singly focused on the problem—*No one disrespects me like that!* or *I'll show them who is in charge!* At other times our thoughts can be quite repetitive when angry, circling around and again over the same issue. Judging others while angry is a good example: *That idiot should know better! How could someone be so stupid? What an idiot. Idiots like that don't deserve what they get.*

Some of this kind of repetition may be about trying to discover a quick way to solve the problem that led to the anger—how does one get others to stop being idiots? This is not necessarily troublesome unless we act on it in a problematic fashion. Other thoughts may be problem-solving shortcuts that can be based on readily accessible information leading to resolution. For instance, if a trusted friend says something that angers you, reminding them they've long had a problem with trusting others can defuse the situation and inspire empathy. However, this shortcut may lead to further difficulties. For instance, when angry, a person may make rapid decisions based on immediate outcomes rather than long-term consequences. Their direct actions may lead to either unhealthy escape or acting out in ways that damage property and relationships.

Certain types of thoughts can also trigger anger. For instance, when you were younger, you might have learned that things should be fair. If you then experience situations in which you encounter unfairness, your anger may be triggered. If you believe that others are not behaving according to principles and rules you learned, or you encounter inequality or injustice, you may find these angering.

We do not mean to say that ideals of fairness aren't important, but that anger can lead people to act in ways that don't serve fairness. We'll explore this more fully in the chapters ahead.

Other thoughts and beliefs can also trigger anger or occur when we're feeling angry:

- Blaming thoughts: holding others responsible for your feelings or for what happens to you; for example, "You cause all of my problems" when the person is likely not the cause of *all* your problems.

- Personalizing thoughts: thinking that matters discussed or explored in a conflict apply specifically to your personality or threaten you as a person rather than being about broader issues. For example, you may believe that someone is calling you incompetent when they are simply talking about a project at work that didn't go well for a multitude of reasons.

- "Being right" thoughts: believing or insisting that your way is the right way while failing to recognize others' opinions and desires; for example, insisting *My way is the best way* when there are actually many and varied ways to do things.

- Labeling or evaluative thoughts: labeling yourself or others as bad, idiotic, or a failure without considering the full context or situation; for instance, *That driver is an idiot for going so fast,* when they may be rushing to deal with an emergency.

- Expectation thoughts: believing that yourself or others should not disappoint you, or that you or they should always measure up to ideals—fuming, for example, *I never thought my partner would act that way; I can't believe he did that!* when a partner acts contrary to your wishes.

These are just a few examples of the types of thoughts that can lead to or sustain anger. Note that having these types of thoughts doesn't mean there is necessarily a problem with your thinking. We are all susceptible to these different ways of thinking from time to time. We all label and evaluate. We all have times when we feel that we are right, or take things personally, or blame others. We all have expectations. This is a natural result of learning, of having a mind that thinks—a subject we'll turn more fully to in chapter 5. For now, we invite you to continue to work on becoming aware of your anger experiences by completing exercise 1.3.

Exercise 1.3: Noticing Your Repeating Thought Patterns When Angry

In the space provided, list the top five thoughts you are aware of when you feel slightly angry or just irritated; for example, *Nobody does this correctly* or *That driver is an idiot*. If any of your top five match one of the kinds of thoughts that trigger or sustain anger listed above, write that in parentheses directly after your thought; for example, *Nobody does this correctly* ("being right" thought) or *That driver is an idiot* (labeling thought).

1. _____

2. _____

3. _____

4. _____

5. _____

Rate the level of anger you need to experience to be aware of these thoughts by circling a number:

1	2	3	4	5

Low levels   High levels

In the space provided, list the top five thoughts you are aware of when you feel very angry—for example, swearing or demanding that others be different or do something. Again, note the type of thought in parentheses after the thought.

1. _____

2. _____

3. _____

4. _____

5. _____

Rate the level of anger you need to experience to be aware of these thoughts by circling a number:

1	2	3	4	5

Low levels   High levels

Actions and the Experience of Anger

Behavioral responses to anger are the most identifiable and problematic. These are the behaviors that seem to be driven by anger and, depending on the behavior, can cause harm, both psychological and physical, to oneself and others. These actions can range from giving someone the cold shoulder to damaging property (breaking things, punching walls) to physically harming oneself or others (hitting, kicking). It can be helpful to explore this range of behaviors by using familiar terms that you likely have heard before.

Aggressive

The first type of action or actions we can take when we're angry is known as *aggressive* behavior. These behaviors are generally easy to identify, as they can often be seen and heard. These also tend to be the most damaging. Those who behave aggressively while angry try to control others or gain control through threatening or physical actions. These behaviors are generally harmful, often leading to lasting emotional, psychological, and potentially physical effects. Aggressive actions might include:

- Physical violence, such as hitting, kicking, biting, shoving, and restraining

- Verbal hostility, such as threatening harm or sending attacking and threatening messages through social media, emails, or texts

- Driving aggressively and dangerously

- Causing property damage, such as throwing objects, punching walls, smashing windows, or damaging vehicles

- Yelling, shouting, or screaming

- Bullying, intimidating, or coercing

- Humiliating others verbally

Aggressive actions serve to intimidate or cow others. These actions often cause fear in others and give the perpetrator a sense of control. However, when you "look" closely at the internal experience of the person who behaves in this fashion, often you may see that they are fearful themselves. We often act in aggressive ways to try to avoid or control our fear or other internal experiences. Ultimately these behaviors are destructive to both the person who engages in them and the recipients. These actions primarily lead to unhealthy interactions, damaged relationships, and long-term suffering.

Passive-Aggressive

A second common term, which is well explored conceptually in psychology, is *passive-aggressive*. Passive-aggressive behaviors or actions are characterized by communicating anger indirectly. The person engaging in these types of behaviors feels upset, but rather than expressing it directly, they use other actions to communicate what they are feeling. Forms of resistance or manipulation often characterize passive-aggressive behaviors. Here are some examples:

- Pouting or showing displeasure by wearing a sullen expression

- Giving the silent treatment or cold shoulder

- Saying that "nothing is wrong" when asked, even though body language indicates otherwise

- Withdrawing or withholding love, affection, or attention

- Being kind to someone's face but gossiping or getting even behind their back

- Refusing to cooperate, or competing when there is no real need for competition

- Tattling on the person they are angry with, to get them in trouble

- Obstructing progress on projects or other activities

- Procrastinating when time is of the essence

- Being sarcastic or giving back-handed compliments (for example, "Hey, that outfit looks good—I didn't think you could carry it off")

Most of us engage in some of these types of behaviors at different times in our lives. We can all be indirect in our communication when feeling angry. However, if we routinely engage in a pattern of passive-aggressive behavior when we feel angry, it can damage our relationships. It can lead the person engaging in these actions to feel ashamed, alone, and isolated.

Passive

Being *passive* is the third action we may take when feeling angry. Rather than communicating anger indirectly, as demonstrated in the examples of passive-aggression above, the person engaging in a purely passive response style tends to avoid conflict and other types of communication about anger altogether. They tend to suppress or repress their anger. Because these actions often involve some sort of escape, the person they are angry with may never even know there is a problem that needs to be addressed. The suppression makes the associated actions difficult to spot; however, some examples might include drinking alcohol or sleeping.

As you read about and consider the different ways that anger can be expressed through actions, be aware that people can engage in a combination of these behaviors. Anger experiences can be complicated, as noted, and different situations and contexts can lead to distinct behavioral responses. The key is to be aware of the actions you take while angry, noting those that do not serve you well and that prevent healthy communication and relationships. We know that you picked up this book for a reason—something's not working when it comes to your anger and how it is expressed.

Exercise 1.4: Noticing Your Actions in Response to Anger

In the space provided, list the top five actions you take when you feel *slightly* angry; for example, sighing heavily or avoiding others.

1. _____

2. _____

3. _____

4. _____

5. _____

Rate the level of anger you need to experience to take these actions by circling a number below:

1	2	3	4	5

Low levels   High levels

In the space provided, list the top five actions you take when you feel *very* angry; for example, throwing objects or giving someone the cold shoulder for an extended period.

1. _____

2. _____

3. _____

4. _____

5. _____

Rate the level of anger you need to experience to take these actions by circling a number below:

1	2	3	4	5

Low levels   High levels

When you become angry, do you engage in aggressive actions, passive-aggressive actions, or passive actions? Or a combination? Comment here.

_____

_____

Where you listed the top five actions you take when slightly angry and very angry, note what type of response it is, by writing next to each action "PA" for a passive-aggressive action, "P" for a passive action, or "A" for an aggressive action. If a behavior falls into more than one category, write all the letters that apply.

Physiology, Thoughts, and Actions: The Full Experience of Anger

Now that you've reviewed the three areas of personal experience involved in feeling anger (physiological sensations, thoughts, and actions), let's revisit the complexity of anger. Depending on the function and context of the anger, you might experience different combinations of physical sensations, thoughts, and actions. You may avoid an angry feeling by going to bed and sleeping; at other times you may act aggressively, pounding your fists on the table. At still other times of anger you may give someone the cold shoulder or be sarcastic. Whatever the combination of experiences, it is most important to look for problematic patterns of behavior while angry and to understand their function.

Problematic Patterns of Behavior When Angry

It bears repeating: Everyone experiences anger. It is a normal response to events that challenge us, involve conflict, or threaten us in some way. To experience and express anger is a part of being alive; it is part of our emotional spectrum. Recognizing our experiences of anger is helpful. Understanding what is happening for you when you feel angry can assist in developing renewed and healthier relationships, better communication, and connection to individuals and groups such as family and coworkers. But fundamentally, understanding your experience of anger can help you identify problematic patterns of behavior that interfere with your own well-being. It will also help you understand problematic interactions with others.

Typically, it is not the single outburst that causes long-standing problems. You can imagine being tired and exhausted at the end of a long workday, driving home, and while driving, yelling at the driver who just cut you off. If this happens from time to time, it may not be that big of a deal in the larger scheme of things. However, if you find yourself yelling at other drivers regularly—if it is a pattern—then your well-being may be at higher risk. Let's look at a few more examples.

Imagine that you and your partner have had an extended period of conflict. You each have been feeling angry at the other. A disagreement has been simmering in the background. You finally have a discussion about it, and you both raise your voices, the problem isn't solved, and then you give each other the cold shoulder for the night. In this example, too, these behaviors and experiences may not be, by themselves, reason for alarm. Most couples experience anger and conflict in their relationships. The issue becomes problematic and potentially damaging if most or every conflict unfolds in this fashion. It's worth noticing the impact on yourself and others, as well as the outcomes. Yelling when angry as a pattern can begin to take its toll.

In another example, let's imagine that a coworker continually interrupts you on a day when you're under a deadline to get a project done. Instead of confronting him, you quietly grow angry and begin to mumble under your breath when you hear him coming down the hall. However, when he enters your office you remain polite, answering his questions and returning to your work as quickly as possible. During his visit and after he leaves, you feel quite irritated but turn back to your work. Silently suppressing anger in this circumstance may not cause more significant problems between you and your coworker. But if you get interrupted at work more routinely, and you begin to quietly seethe about the interruptions, trouble may lie ahead. Stress at work may increase, and relationships and productivity may start to suffer.

We hope that with these few examples you can start to recognize actions when you're angry that primarily may not be problematic, as they occur only now and then. The repeated behavioral reactions are the ones that lead to ongoing difficulties, including not living and behaving in a way that you would like or is effective for you. As well, these habitual responses can lead to emotional and psychological fallout. This fallout might include not getting your needs met, other relationship problems, feeling ashamed, or having negative and critical thoughts about yourself and others.

Finally, it is worth noting that violent actions when you're angry can be problematic even if it happens only once. Behaving violently almost always leads to suffering and almost always has negative consequences, if not immediately, then ultimately. It is a bigger problem if you or people you know engage in violence in a habitual way; that is, if you or others routinely turn to violence when angry, then the fallout is significant and likely harmful to all involved. Think back to Angela and Jerold from the beginning of the chapter as examples of long-term fallout. Angela was often taken advantage of and rarely stood her ground in times of her own need. Jerold struggled to form lasting and supportive relationships. Violence nearly always exacts a very high cost.

Exercise 1.5: Patterns of Action When Angry

In the space provided, write any patterns that you notice regarding your reactions or actions taken when you feel angry; for example, "When I am angry, I often *withdraw* and stop talking to people" or "When I am angry, I tend to *use curse words* a fair amount."

_____

_____

_____

_____

_____

_____

The Function of Anger

We have looked at physiological responses to anger, thoughts when angry, and actions when angry. We have also looked at patterns of behavior when angry. But what is the *function* of anger? This is probably the most critical question to explore when it comes to characterizing or understanding your anger. Knowing how it functions for you, in particular, will also point to ways that you can change your behavior when you're feeling angry, to better serve your values.

Let's define what we mean by *function*. We want to know what purpose the anger might serve. Often the feelings and actions of anger function to protect us against some kind of emotional vulnerability or help us avoid it. Some of us try to control our internal experience of hurt, anxiety, and pain by escaping it with angry behavior. Such angry acting out can also function to neutralize a threat to our ego or self-conceptualization. Our egos and self-conceptions are often linked to vulnerable emotional experiences as well.

One way to understand the function of anger further is to consider its relationship to what came before and after the angry experience. Jerold, from the beginning of the chapter, regularly acts on his anger with aggression. When he feels vulnerable, it feels threatening, and he then behaves aggressively. This behavior helps him avoid feeling vulnerable, and he seems to be back in control. Let's say that Jerold felt humiliated by a friend (what came before the anger, or the *antecedent*), and, in that moment, being unwilling to experience that emotion, he rapidly became angry and smashed a lamp (angry *action* or behavior). After breaking the lamp, Jerold felt more in control, and the friend felt afraid and apologized (what came after, or the *consequence*).

Understanding the function of behavior thus involves looking for what came right before (antecedent), what happened behaviorally (action), and what came right after the angry episode (consequence). Here we can again turn to patterns of angry behavior. Often similar actions (escaping the emotion by engaging in angry behavior) follow similar antecedents (being emotionally triggered) and similar consequences (feelings of relief, feeling in control, people backing away, and so on).

We have given only the single example of Jerold's anger patterns here; anger may function in different ways, depending on the situation. We'll explore this topic further in chapter 2. For instance, anger may serve to stop something terrible from happening. A parent may yell loudly and in anger at a speeding car that has just zoomed down the road where they live. For a parent with small children, this anger may be about protection. Still, you can also see how the parent would feel personally vulnerable. In this case, the angry behavior is likely justifiable. Sometimes angry behavior is about safety. Feeling anger can also motivate people to take action that supports justice. There are numerous examples of this sort. What's essential is understanding how anger is functioning in *your* life.

Exercise 1.6: How Your Anger Functions for You

Referring to your responses to exercise 1.4, in the following table's middle column, labeled "action or behavior," write the five actions you take when slightly angry as well as the five actions you take when you're very angry. Now take a few moments to reflect on the times when you've felt angry and engaged in these behaviors. See if you can identify what came before and what came after the anger experience and behavior. Take your time to be sure; be honest with yourself about what was happening. Note whether you felt emotionally vulnerable in some way. See if you can label what that vulnerability might have been (for example, hurt, anxious, sad, or humiliated). Write that in the left-hand column. In the far right column, labeled "What happened afterward," write what followed the anger or the consequences of the anger. This will help you identify anger's different functions in your life. We understand that it won't always be straightforward. We provide an example in the first row to help you get the gist of the exercise. Do your best and don't worry if it isn't exactly the full story. It is also okay if some of the antecedents and consequences are the same across the behaviors. The main idea is to note what actions occur, then to realize what happens right before, and to be aware of the consequences.

	What came before (antecedent)	Action or behavior (from exercise 1.4)	What happened afterward (consequence)
	I felt hurt when my husband left the dishes in the sink again, and I had thoughts that he just doesn't care about me or the way our house looks.	Washing the dishes in a passive–aggressive manner, sighing heavily, and slamming the cupboards as I put dishes away.	I felt better because the dishes were done, and I had made my point. However, I continued to struggle through the evening, giving my husband the cold shoulder. He later apologized, and that seemed to smooth things out.
1			
2			
3			

4		
5		
6		
7		
8		
9		
10		

As we continue through the book, we'll further explore antecedents, actions, and consequences. We'll help you understand where to make a change so you're no longer a slave to emotional vulnerability. And we'll look at how you can instead choose how to behave in ways that matter most to you. If you're unsure what we are referring to here, no worries; we'll delve fully into these ideas as you read on. You'll learn that emotions of hurt and vulnerability are not that easy to control. Still, behavior or actions can be controlled, helping you feel back in charge of your life in a way that supports well-being.

The Character of Anger at the Social Level

We want to reiterate that anger is a normal, natural emotion that is experienced by virtually all human beings. At times, anger has functional value for survival and is thus part of what helps humans stay alive. In a social context, anger can be a way to mobilize resources. Anger can empower us to intervene when harmful behaviors cause problems in social groups. Anger can also mobilize people around social justice issues. Used appropriately in these circumstances, anger can help restore fairness for, or fair relations among, individuals and societies; for instance, to right an imbalance in social privilege. Anger can motivate productive social movement and change. We'll turn more fully to these types of issues in chapter 11, and explore the cultural differences in anger.

In the remainder of this chapter, we want to briefly cover one other characteristic of anger that's relevant to understanding its nature and impact: the health effects of anger.

Health Effects of Chronic Anger

Several adverse health effects can be caused by chronic anger. These can include a range of problems often related to the relationship between anger and stress. Periods of unhealthy stress can actually lead to anger. They may make you more prone to experiences like road rage, workplace difficulties or violence, or anger at home and in relationships.

The different health effects of chronic stress and anger may include the following:

- Anxiety

- Depression

- Digestion problems

- Insomnia

- Heart attack

- High blood pressure

- Skin problems, such as eczema

- Stroke

Knowing how anger impacts your health can be a motivator for change. The key antidote is learning to express your anger in healthy ways. Managing stress may be part of this process. However, understanding anger and how it impacts your emotional, psychological, and physical health is the focus of this book and the work we'll turn to in the coming chapters.

Treating Problematic Behavior Related to Anger

The main goal of this book is to help you find healthy ways to express anger. Working with and managing your anger practically and sustainably is what we hope to achieve. Let's look more closely at this issue. A recent review of the research literature on the treatment of anger (Lee & DiGiuseppe, 2018) found that cognitive behavioral interventions are most common. These are at least moderately effective for treating problematic anger as well.

Cognitive behavioral approaches focus on many issues but generally attempt to modify a person's behavior by addressing factors that lead to the target behavior—in this case, anger. Unfortunately, treatment for aggressive behavior has been less successful. However, there is hope if a person experiencing aggression is motivated to change. If you're aggressive when angry, you'll need motivation to handle things differently. One of our goals here is to help with motivation as well.

We want to support every reader in expressing their anger in effective ways in line with their personal values. Whether the target angry behavior is aggressive, passive-aggressive, passive, or even somewhere in between, we have tools for you. We believe the most fundamental approach to overcoming the damaging effects of anger involves what the person experiencing it hopes to achieve. The most relevant questions are: What is the meaning you want to create in life? and What values do you most want to live? Your answers are your motivators.

Summary

In this chapter, we have defined anger, illustrating its two poles with the stories of Jerold and Angela. We looked at the varied character of anger and your expression of it. The exercises helped you understand how you express anger through multiple components of the emotion—how it may feel to you and how you think when angry. You also learned about the different forms of anger and its function. Anger can be both a normal, healthy part of being human and a problem that interferes with leading a fulfilling, satisfying life and can lead to serious health consequences. We're here to help you reduce the suffering caused by anger and give you the tools to relate to your anger in a new and healthy way.

We'll be doing this by using a newer cognitive behavioral treatment, acceptance and commitment therapy (ACT). As you'll learn in the following chapter, ACT uses both mindfulness and present-moment processes as well as behavior change and commitment processes to support you in making the change you would like to see. You'll learn how you can choose to express your anger in a way that's appropriate to the situation *and* aligned with your values.

CHAPTER 2

Understanding Change: Acceptance and Commitment Therapy

The first step toward change is awareness. The second step is acceptance.

—Nathaniel Branden

Veronica describes herself as someone who angers easily, getting angry in many different situations. She also fights with her anger, even becoming mad about the anger itself. She came to feel that something was truly wrong with her. She spent significant time and energy trying to control this emotion.

Tired of feeling tense, stiff, and on edge, Veronica decided to see a therapist. During sessions, the therapist noticed that Veronica's tone of voice nearly always felt forced, a part of Veronica's anger expression. Veronica said she was active most of the day, trying to stay busy as it seemed to keep her from getting hijacked by her anger. She expressed difficulty controlling her anger despite her efforts.

Veronica was surprised when her therapist did something unexpected. Instead of focusing on eliminating anger, they worked together to do the opposite. Veronica and her therapist began to explore anger. They unpacked its potential origins and the hurt that was often covered over by the anger. They turned toward the anger, welcoming it as a part of her experience.

Through this work, Veronica began to track where and when she felt angry. She learned about the situations that triggered her anger, realizing that it almost always happened in interpersonal situations where she felt ignored. In these situations, she often thought that she wasn't genuinely heard and acknowledged by someone important to her. She noticed how small and insignificant she felt in those moments.

As they continued to explore Veronica's anger, they learned that she got angry in other interpersonal contexts where she felt invisible as well. This included anger at car drivers who would accidentally cut her off, waiters at restaurants who didn't serve her right away, and friends who didn't immediately return her calls. In each case, again, she felt small and insignificant.

This discovery process wasn't easy for Veronica. She had to focus on her experience, track her anger, and notice what came before and after. Veronica also realized that her anger allowed her to "feel bigger and more powerful." When she used a loud voice and angry expression, she momentarily felt relief from feeling ignored. When angry, she was "seen" by others. It turned out that anger was not her enemy, but a way of responding to not being seen. As psychologist Marshall B. Rosenberg would say, her expression of anger was a tragic expression of an unmet need.

Context Matters

As Veronica explored the situations where she became angry, she realized the fuller story of her anger and its costs. In the *context* of interpersonal relationships where Veronica felt ignored, she experienced negative emotions that she didn't like. To avoid these experiences, she reacted with anger. This behavior worked in the short term but failed in the long term, leading to a greater struggle with her internal experience.

Veronica came to understand through therapy that by getting angry she was moving away from vulnerability. She was engaged in an unhealthy pattern of avoidance of her own emotions—she was nonaccepting of what she felt.

By looking at the context and the function, we can see that her anger is only a symptom of a more significant problem. Veronica was unwilling to feel vulnerable. When you begin to understand the context and function of your anger, you'll be able to more easily identify what to do. This will make things better concerning the fallout of your anger.

To continue exploring Veronica's journey, recall how we visited the function of anger in chapter 1, and you completed exercise 1.6 to look at the antecedent, the angry behavior, and the consequence. Applying this to Veronica's story, we can better understand the function of her anger: to avoid feeling ignored, small, or insignificant. For Veronica, the antecedent was being ignored in an interpersonal situation (the context) where she would then feel small or insignificant; the behavior she engaged in was to become loud and powerful; and the consequence was being heard and seen (the function) in the interpersonal interaction.

Now, you might say, "Good for Veronica!" She is getting what she wants by becoming angry. And you would be right concerning the short-term consequences. In the immediate aftermath of her angry behavior, she would get attention—no longer being ignored. However, if we look at the long-term consequences of her behavior, a different story emerges.

As Veronica continued to act in this fashion, those around her began to feel annoyed and sometimes anxious; ultimately, they began to withdraw. Veronica was losing relationships vital to her. And with this loss, her feelings of being unheard, small, and insignificant grew.

If Veronica is willing to experience feeling vulnerable (small and insignificant) in the context of an interpersonal relationship in which she feels ignored, she may be able to make changes. Rather than trying to control or avoid these experiences by becoming angry, she can open herself to responding in alternative ways that are more workable in the long term. We'll continue to explore what is meant here as we work through the chapters on ACT processes, but for now, let's see if we can discover even more about your anger by looking at the situations in which it occurs.

Exercise 2.1: Knowing the Context of Your Anger

In this exercise, we'll shine an investigative light on the context of your anger and the long-term consequences. Complete the table by filling in examples from your life that give the details of your anger experiences. We provide an example to help you get started. Try to list varied situations to understand the emotions you may be avoiding or the underlying need that's not being met. After completing the table, answer the questions that follow.

Context				
Situation	**Thoughts and sensations**	**Action**	**Immediate/ short-term consequence**	**Long-term consequence**
My partner was late to pick me up from work.	*She doesn't care about me. She is inconsiderate.* *She is selfish.* Tension in my shoulders, tightness in my stomach. Red face.	I paced angrily at the corner where she picks me up and then yelled at her when she finally arrived.	Promises from my partner that she will not be late again. Apologies from my partner. I feel in control again.	Over time, as I continue to yell in these situations, my partner gets angry and we begin to fight more. Eventually the relationship breaks down.

Context		Action	Immediate/ short-term consequence	Long-term consequence
Situation	Thoughts and sensations			

1. Do you find a pattern to the situations (contexts) where you get angry? In which situations do you most often get angry (for instance, interpersonal relationships where you feel ignored)?

    _____

    _____

    _____

2. How do you usually feel after an angry outburst or attempt to suppress anger?

    _____

    _____

    _____

3. What do you notice about the difference between short-term and long-term consequences? How is the anger functioning in your life?

    _____

    _____

    _____

We hope that by completing this exercise you discovered that anger functions for you in a particular way, given a specific context. Indeed, in the context of control of internal experience through avoidance and angry behavior, it may even be considered useful. When Veronica got angry, she got to escape feeling vulnerable or insignificant. However, even if beneficial in the moment—her anger led her to be seen—the long-term costs were too high, and perhaps even the short-term costs were too high.

Looking closely at what is typically being avoided, you can sense that something important is needed. Veronica needed or wanted attention from others. She wanted to be acknowledged and respected. She tried to not feel invisible in her interpersonal relationships, but did it in an ineffective way. In this case the anger was much like a yellow light at an intersection; it was signaling something. Perhaps it is time for you to see what your anger might be signaling.

Following the tenets of ACT, you'll look to this signal, seeing what is needed, and then, working through this book, begin to develop a different relationship with the inner landscape of your experience. Instead of a narrow focus perpetuated by rules about what is okay to feel, you'll work to broaden your experience. This will allow you to express a wider range of emotions and begin to choose behaviors that take you toward the long-term consequences you desire. As with watering seeds you have sown, what you nurture regularly and carefully will respond and grow. Watering unwise expressions of anger causes its own difficulties, raising a garden of thorny weeds. By watering different seeds—seeds of acceptance—you'll cultivate the kind of garden you would like to see grow: alive and thriving with the vibrant colors of your values.

We'll continue to consider and explore the feeling and context of anger. Now let's take a closer look at why ACT focuses on the acceptance of internal experience.

The Human Mind

The human mind is fascinating. It has the power to create and imagine. It can problem solve and remember. It can be quite busy, seeming to go in many different directions at once, or it can focus steadily on a single thing for some time. The human mind collects and stores a wealth of knowledge, individually and collectively; with this complex tool we have created a vast store of knowledge in books, computers, and other devices, as well as technological advances that have built the civilization we live in today.

One other interesting thing about our minds is their eternal nature—continually operating, engaging in an ongoing commentary on all that we do. You can quickly check this everlasting quality of ongoing thinking by simply asking yourself to not have a thought. Try to not think or have a thought. What do you notice? If you're like most humans, you will see that not thinking for more than a brief moment is a near impossibility. Now you might ask, "What about when I am sleeping?" Fair enough. Perhaps you're not thinking while sleeping, but how would you know? You're asleep! And we do know this: your mind often dreams while sleeping, creating images and stories even when you're unconscious to your surroundings. The mind, like all things human, is in motion. Your heart is continuously beating, your blood is always flowing, your cells are growing and dying, your gut is digesting, your lungs are breathing—and your mind is thinking.

Thought after thought after thought flows ceaselessly through your mind. The next exercise will raise your awareness of this fact.

Exercise 2.2: Watching Thinking

Begin by finding a quiet place to sit. Plan to sit there silently for about five minutes.

1.   Once you are seated, take a big breath in and out and then begin to notice what you're thinking about. See if you can notice that your mind is producing thought after thought. Let your thoughts

simply flow. Notice how many different things you think about in five minutes and how there doesn't really seem to be much space between thoughts.

2. Now, in the space provided, write about what you noticed your thoughts were "saying" as you did this exercise.

_____

_____

_____

_____

3. Now repeat the exercise, but this time focus your mind on a time when you were angry. Let your thoughts simply flow about that period of anger. What thoughts were you having then? Notice how many different thoughts you had. Notice whether the thoughts you had while angry were repetitive.

4. In the space provided, write about what you noticed your thoughts were "saying" as you focused on a time when you were angry.

_____

_____

_____

_____

Whether we're angry or not angry, thoughts continuously flow. They are always on the move, even if they are repetitive.

So we know two things about the human mind: (1) it thinks, and (2) it thinks all the time. Our thinking includes all symbolic behavior, like imagining or picturing in your mind's eye or body language. We start to think at a very young age. Our vocabulary and ability to imagine grow over time until we become fully thinking, imagining adults. Our knowledge grows, and we become so good at thinking that we forget that we once knew only one or two words to express all we were thinking, like "Mama" or "Baba." We learn so well, and our language becomes so powerfully developed that it can seem like we were always able to think the thoughts that occupy our minds today.

It is helpful to remember that we had to learn this symbolic behavior called thinking, and that the way we think is, in part, a product of our learning environment. Genes and biology also play a role. Our thinking is a product of a complex interplay of biology, genetics, and straightforward learning. However, it is our learning history that is most relevant to the work we are doing here. For instance, your mind has learned some thoughts about anger and how it should be displayed. Part of your work in this book will be about beginning to notice that you're always thinking. This will prove useful as we move forward and will become a part of acceptance.

What We Have Learned with Our Minds Matters

The "library" of your mind is vast; you have tons of information in your mind that is fluidly boiling around as you think. Some of this information is about how to be in the world and includes rules for behaving in socially appropriate ways. It also includes rules about anger. You learn rules, and these are verbal, like "Look both ways before you cross the street." This rule is now a thought and part of our thinking. You can respond to or follow this rule with your behavior by doing as it says.

Rules also connect with many other related thoughts and related forms of behavior. For instance, when you were young you likely learned: "Be polite." Your mind can think that thought and other thoughts about what it means to be polite—*It's kind to be polite, Being polite is good,* and even *I hate being polite.* If you're following the rule—be polite—then you're doing things like not interrupting others while they are speaking and saying "please" when asking for something. You are waiting for your turn in public lines and the like.

Being able to follow the rules of common courtesy is quite helpful for trying to get along in society. It can guide our behavior in ways that are useful and effective in relationships.

We learn thousands upon thousands of rules—indeed, we can make our own rules, through thinking—about how to be in the world. On the whole, learning rules and following rules is important and keeps us functioning as a social group. However, there are some rules and ways of behaving concerning them that can lead to problems. Not every rule is healthy, and some, when followed blindly, can be harmful.

When it comes to anger, some rules that you learned from your upbringing and some rules that you made yourself can lead to trouble if you act on them. For instance, if you have a rule that you're "always right," it is likely to cause a fair bit of argument or a need to bite your tongue and suffer silently. Other rules are about how you should feel and what you should feel. Indeed, rules about anger and emotions, in general, can lead to more significant problems when misapplied or excessively applied. The rules you have learned come about through the process of learning to think. Rules are a part of thinking, and these rules matter. They help or hinder the way you live your life.

The Rule of Excessive and Misapplied Control

As children, we are taught to think about our emotions. We not only learn the names for our feelings (we label them using language), but we also learn about how to relate to them when they show up. We learn to sort our emotions into particular categories. To get a sense of what we mean by this, complete exercise 2.3.

Exercise 2.3: Emotion Sort

In the following table, place a "G" next to the emotion word if it is generally viewed as a *good* emotion and a "B" next to the emotion word if it is generally viewed as a *bad* emotion.

Emotion	Good or Bad	Emotion	Good or Bad
Anxiety		Anger	
Contentment		Happiness	
Outrage		Vexation	
Love		Awe	
Fear		Boredom	
Bliss		Frustration	
Annoyance		Fury	
Bitterness		Calm	
Peacefulness		Resentment	
Irritability		Offense	
Sorrow		Joy	

You may have noticed that we included a fair number of the words from the chapter 1 Words for Describing Anger list. Have you identified most of these anger words as good or bad? We suspect they got a B. We also imagine that it wasn't difficult to sort the emotions, although we understand that it isn't always clear cut. Depending on the *context* and *function* of the emotion, you might consider it good—healthy, normal, even an essential component of your emotional spectrum.

Although we both believe that emotions are neither good nor bad per se—that they simply are what they are—we still live in a world where emotions tend to be divvied up this way. This comes into play when we consider our relationship to these categories. When something is "bad," human beings typically support the idea that they should get rid of it. This applies to anger directly. If we don't like something because it is bad, we reason that we should figure out how to make it go away. You can begin to get a sense of the rule that is coming into play: Get rid of bad stuff = get rid of your anger.

Throughout our lives we learn that the emotions designated bad or negative, including anger, should be controlled or eliminated as quickly as possible. We learn this rule specifically: control your emotions (especially the bad ones). This rule can come in many forms; for instance, you may have learned that when you feel sad, you "should get over it." Or you may have learned when you feel anxious to "just not think about it." Or you may have learned that when you're angry, you should not show it, or it becomes an emotion to cover up or hide other feelings.

The problem with this rule—"control your emotions"—is that often this is impossible. It is tough to not feel what we feel! Indeed, you usually have to feel it first to know that you want to control it. It's a paradox. Hiding anger doesn't make it go away. And using anger to hide other emotions doesn't make them go away either.

We get stuck in applying a rule in ways that don't work for us—that is, we misapply control to our emotions. And we often do this to excess. This type of control paradoxically leads to all kinds of other problems. We'll take a deep dive into this issue of problematic control in chapter 3. For now, it is critical to understand that this kind of control causes more significant problems, and it is the opposite of acceptance.

Here we have come full circle. The problems that emerge from excessive and misapplied control of emotions (as well as thoughts and sensations) are significant and are likely part of why you have picked up this book. The rule about needing to be in control of your emotions can actually lead you to feel out of control. Perhaps you understand what we mean when you consider your own anger behaviors. Do you feel in control? If yes, for how long and at what cost?

Acceptance, then, is an alternative to control. Remember, though, we are still just starting our journey through this book. You may be saying to yourself, *But being out of control with my anger—by hiding it or inappropriately acting on it—is precisely my problem. I need more control.* Rest assured that we'll look closely at the paradox of control shortly. More specifically, we'll consider how control is related to anger. But we'll be looking at two types of control: control of your internal experience (emotions, thoughts, and sensations) and control of your behavior. With the former, we'll be exploring acceptance; with the latter, we'll be exploring commitment.

The Model of ACT

ACT works by looking at how people relate to their mind and its rules. As such, it focuses on our relationship with our inner world and how that relationship manifests in our behavior. ACT uses the six core processes described in the introduction to change problematic relationships with inner experiences, so that a person's suffering related to these experiences diminishes.

Suffering and Anger

When we act on our anger in ways that cause personal and interpersonal problems, it can lead to a great deal of suffering. Let's take the example of Richard. Richard was very avoidant of feelings of hurt and shame. In his young years, he had learned rules that it was not okay for males to express feelings of pain or shame. He had learned that these emotions were weak and vulnerable and should not be shared. In his early adult years, Richard got married—and as could be expected, from time to time his wife would say or do something hurtful to him. Instead of talking about these hurt feelings, he would lash out in anger, sometimes breaking things in the house and sometimes shoving his wife to the floor. She eventually tired of this behavior and left the relationship. Richard, hurt by her leaving, continued to be angry and became even more aggressive in his next relationship. This one ended as well.

As the years passed, Richard was in and out of relationships, each failing as he lashed out angrily again and again. Not only did his partners suffer at the hands of the abusive behavior, but Richard suffered as well. He felt lonely and hurt quite often. He was ashamed that he couldn't maintain a relationship, and he was ashamed of his behavior. Richard's suffering grew over time. He kept telling himself that he needed to get himself under control, not recognizing that there were two issues of control at hand. One, however, was about letting go of control and accepting his feelings of hurt and shame rather than covering them up with anger. The other was about getting in control of his behavior, aligning his behavior with his values.

Almost everyone suffers when they act on anger in ways inconsistent with their values. They also suffer when they try to run away from or escape other important emotions by using anger as a form of avoidance. There are many ways we act on or in anger that can cause suffering; you may recognize some of them among these examples:

- Dwelling on past instances of anger, showing resentment, or worrying about how you will handle anger in the future; wanting to take revenge or make someone, including yourself, pay for something that led to the anger

- Avoiding emotions, thoughts, sensations, people, places, and things that evoke anger, making your life smaller and more unlivable

- Fusing or getting entangled with thoughts and stories about what you or others should or should not have done in angry situations, or fusing with stories about how others should act or treat you, or thoughts about who is right and who is wrong

- Viewing yourself as an angry person and then continually expressing and experiencing this self-assessment, not being open to new or different perspectives that could be helpful

- Moving away from what you care about or find meaningful in life because you're angry about something

- Creating destructive outcomes such as ruined relationships, damaged reputations, or painful conflicts caused by the angry behavior you engage in

Let's look more closely at the suffering that you experience due to anger. As you write about suffering in exercise 2.4, notice whether it is linked to or caused by the patterns of angry behavior you wrote about in chapter 1. Also notice whether the functions of anger you wrote about in chapter 1, however useful they may be for changing things in the short term (for instance, the cold shoulder gets someone to apologize), actually lead to a long-term negative impact (for example, always giving the cold shoulder harms the relationship). Indeed, the long-term adverse effects may be the suffering itself.

Exercise 2.4: Your Personal Suffering

In the space provided, write about the ways you have experienced personal suffering as a result of your anger. Consider how it has impacted you and your sense of well-being as well as how it has affected others. Note whether it has caused loneliness, growing anger, or other forms of suffering for yourself. Write freely—no need to worry about punctuation or getting it perfect. Simply let yourself explore through writing the suffering you have experienced due to angry behavior.

_____

_____

_____

_____

_____

_____

_____

With the work in this book, we are interested in decreasing your suffering that is the result of anger. We focus on assisting you in finding a different way to relate to your emotions, thoughts, and sensations—in this case, those associated explicitly with anger—to regain the life you would like to live. A life that is values-oriented and meaningful. A life that reduces suffering and grows opportunity for well-being. Let's take a brief look at how ACT will help you do this.

The Six Core Processes of ACT

ACT has six interrelated processes that support healthy change. These processes are intimately tied together and, taken as a whole, can help you create the life you want: living with anger but not acting on it in harmful ways.

As you read about these six core processes, begin to consider what they might mean for you and your relationship with anger. Notice whether any of the processes are completely new to you, or perhaps sound familiar but calling for a refresher. Either way, you will have the opportunity to take a deep dive into the processes, as individual chapters concerning each and how we'll apply them to anger lie ahead. The upcoming chapters will go into richer detail about how you can use these processes to relate to your anger differently, building a life that you want instead of suffering at the hands of anger. In the meantime, reflect on each process as you read, considering how it might play a role in your journey to change your relationship to anger.

ACCEPTANCE

Acceptance is the alternative to excessive and misapplied control of your internal experience. Control typically functions to narrow your attention to focusing on "the problem"—namely, your anger and what is causing it. This narrowing reduces flexibility and may actually enhance or sustain anger. In contrast, acceptance—willingness to experience thoughts, feelings, and sensations—broadens your range of response or action alternatives to anger, allowing you to pursue other behaviors.

Put another way, when you're more open to your emotions, anger is less likely to take over. There is no need to keep following the familiar rule about eliminating or controlling anger. Choice becomes available, freeing you to act differently than you might typically act. The goal is to create a context of openness, experiencing all thoughts, emotions, and sensations fully and without defense.

Willingness to experience involves an active process that serves a self-defined purpose. With acceptance, suffering is decreased by allowing your naturally elicited response, letting it be what it is: a thought, a feeling, a sensation, a memory. This work is done *compassionately*; it is not intended to diminish experience, but instead be present to and acknowledge it.

DEFUSION

Defusion is about creating a sense of perspective concerning your thoughts. The defusion process is designed to help you specifically target and reconsider the social and contextual supports for thoughts as causes of behavior. You *have* thoughts; you are not the thoughts themselves, including your thoughts related to anger. Defusion works by changing the context so the ongoing process of thinking is more evident. Defusion gives you a chance to interact with language in nonliteral ways—seeing words for what they are—sounds that refer to an object. They are not the object itself. More on this to come!

PRESENT MOMENT

Behavior can be disproportionately influenced by the past or future. When you get stuck in what happened or worry about what is to come, you lose the experience that is happening in this moment. Present-moment work broadens your personal context beyond what your mind is saying about what was or what might be. Present-moment orientation opens the door for additional cues in the current environment to influence your behavior. You can respond to what is here and now instead of what was in the past. Living more fully in the moment can free you to be in the here and now instead of there and then.

SELF-AS-CONTEXT

Coming into contact with a sense of self that is larger than any single internal experience can help you connect to the ongoing flow of your thoughts, feelings, and sensations. It can also help you contact a sense of self open to different perspectives. Viewing yourself as a matter of perspective: I/here/now helps you "see" that you are *an experiencer*, not merely *what is experienced*. This sense of an observing self is beyond evaluation and cannot be easily described, as it has no parts or pieces and lies outside of narrow rules and logic. It is a felt sense that is conscious awareness itself.

VALUES

Clarifying and defining your values creates a sense of life meaning and direction while allowing you more functional flexibility compared to following concrete or ineffective rules. Your values are determined by your behavior, not necessarily by private content such as thoughts and feelings. You choose and live your values in each moment. Still, they stretch into the future, guiding your life as you move through time.

COMMITTED ACTION

Committed action is about engaging in behavior that aligns with your values. The goal here is to help you build ever-larger patterns of that kind of behavior. With committed action, the everyday activities you engage in help you create purpose and meaning in your life.

The Three Pillars of ACT: Open, Aware, Engaged

Taken all together, the six core processes in ACT will work to help you gain more mental and emotional flexibility. Acceptance and defusion create openness; contact with the present moment and self-as-context support awareness; and values and committed action lead to engagement. The ultimate goal is to live in a way that brings to life the three pillars of ACT—*open, aware,* and *engaged.* As you continue with your quest to change your relationship to anger, keep these pillars in mind: you are building an open, aware, and engaged life.

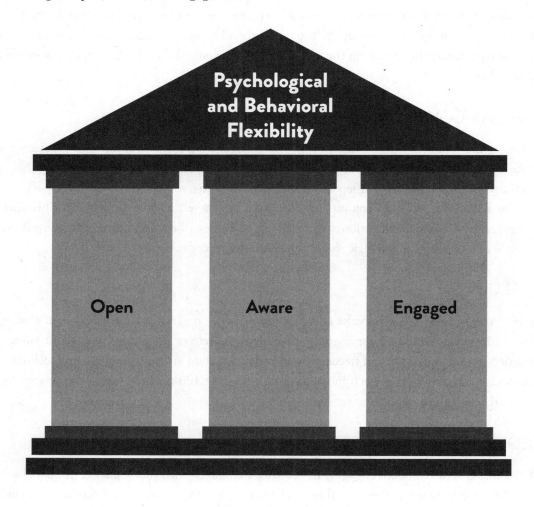

Summary

We learn to think at a very young age. In so doing, we also learn to categorize our emotions as good and bad, and we develop rules about how to be. These rules can be helpful, but they can also lead to problems. One rule, for instance, to control your emotion or get rid of what is labeled as "bad," can lead us to try and eliminate emotions—in this case, anger. However, control applied to your internal experience only expands and complicates the experience. Beginning to understand the purpose of ACT will set the stage for understanding how to relate to your anger and associated emotions, thoughts, and sensations in a healthy way. Becoming open, aware, and engaged is the long-term solution to the immediate problems that anger can engender. You can increase your openness by recognizing acceptance as an active process—being willing to experience internal events as well as defusing from what your mind has to say when it is useful to do so. You can build awareness and make room for choice by starting to connect to your experience in the moment while contacting a sense of self that is more than the identity or story of anger. Choice allows values-based behaviors to come alive as you engage in creating an engaged, meaningful, and purposeful life.

As we press forward in the book, we invite you to challenge yourself, working with each of the chapters fully, completing the exercises, and committing to behavior change. We don't think it will always be easy. Confronting some parts of yourself may be challenging. But we believe that your journey with ACT will make a positive difference for you as you shift from being controlled by anger to being engaged in meaningful activities linked to your values. Onward!

CHAPTER 3

Letting Go of Control:
What Works and What Does Not

One should...be able to see things as hopeless and yet be determined to make them otherwise.

—F. Scott Fitzgerald

Joseph usually appears to others to be a quiet person. Outwardly, he seems mild-mannered—an easygoing guy. Inwardly, however, Joseph's experience is a different story. If others could see his inner world, they would see that it's filled with struggle. Joseph often experiences turmoil. He is engaged in thoughts of comparison and feelings of frustration. He continually evaluates his behavior in relationship to others, typically thinking that he does things correctly while others do not; that he is right, and they are all wrong.

Joseph is routinely hijacked by these thoughts about others and how they should be doing things better or the way *he* does. And just like kindling added to a fire, these critical thoughts fuel the flames of anger. This leads to several difficulties. When Joseph drives alone, for instance, he explodes at other drivers, yelling at them from behind the car window's safety, regularly shouting how they should drive correctly. At work, he often seethes quietly, criticizing others internally for not doing things efficiently or courteously—the way *he* does. This internal anger leads to a fair amount of suffering for Joseph. Because others are never good enough, he is often alone.

Joseph's anger is most painful in the arena of love. He is never long in a relationship. Sooner or later, his partner does something "wrong," and he no longer keeps his anger inside. He either explodes or behaves in passive-aggressive ways toward his partner. Ultimately, the relationship ends. The challenge is Joseph's understanding of this problem. He assumes the world is a complicated place, not fitting into his ideas about how it should be. Joseph fails to recognize that the world is imperfect and will never follow his standards. Letting go of his thoughts about how the world and others should be was Joseph's most significant therapy challenge.

Anger and Workability

Anger is natural; it can be a sensible response to a given situation, one necessary for your survival. Depending on how you relate to anger, it may even help you flourish. But if you get hooked by anger, it can lead to significant personal and collective suffering. In this chapter, we explore patterns of reaction to anger and their costs. We'll look closely at what works when we experience feelings of anger and what does not. We'll begin to explore what it means to let go.

Joseph found therapy challenging, but he continued treatment in the service of finding lasting love. It wasn't easy for him to open his eyes to the consequences of holding too tightly to his stories and ideas about how others should behave. He struggled to let go of his unrelenting standards about right and wrong and to discover how he was participating in his own suffering. Joseph learned that his attempts to control others' behavior were actually attempts to control his own feelings of inadequacy. This took courage, as well as patience.

Using Joseph as an example of the potentially challenging work that lies ahead, we invite you to be patient. We recognize that as you work to find new ways to relate to your anger, you may need to dwell in uncomfortable places. For some, it's hard to discover that they are actually hiding feelings of inadequacy or vulnerability, and that their attempts to control their thoughts and emotions related to anger are excessive and misapplied.

Given the challenge of letting go of control, it is essential to remember that discomfort precedes growth. But when you're seeking transformation, there is no more natural way. Take time to recognize that behavior change is a process—it takes effort and time. Be gentle along the way. We are headed somewhere with the work in this book, and we think you will find the journey valuable. When you learn how to pause and connect honestly with your inner experience, you may be able to unhook, open to experience, and respond more wisely. Letting go and finding your way to a life that works without being hijacked by anger will be part of this voyage.

Let's look first at what getting hijacked by anger does to you and for you.

Anger as a Form of Control

In chapter 2 we talked about excessive and misapplied control of internal experience. Human beings learn that they should control their thoughts and emotions, especially if they are considered "bad" or negative. When it comes to anger, this kind of control can be a two-pronged struggle. First, because anger is one of the emotions that is often seen as bad or negative, we are asked to control it. But as noted, it is not the *emotion* of anger itself that is problematic; rather, it's the behavior you engage in while angry that leads to problems, and indeed that very behavior may need to be controlled. There is anger the feeling, and anger the behavior or action. *This distinction is crucial.* Again, it's the angry behavior (for example, throwing things, hitting, pushing, and other forms of acting out) that we are interested in helping you to control.

The second prong? Anger itself is a form of control, whether we're acting out in anger or suppressing it. We regularly use our anger responses to hide or cover up our more vulnerable emotions and their related thoughts and sensations. For instance, Joseph was using anger to cover or control his feelings of inadequacy. Veronica, from chapter 2, used anger to avoid feeling invisible, small, or insignificant. Jerold, from chapter 1, used anger to hide his feelings of fear and humiliation.

Again, people who struggle with anger usually do one of two things when hijacked by anger: act out or suppress. In both chapters 1 and 2, we explored questions about the function of anger, such as, "What is anger in the service of?" and "What is the purpose of my angry behavior?" We'll now look at the function of angry behavior, whether it includes acting out or suppression.

When you're trying to let go of your attempts to control your acting out or suppression of anger, step one is identifying the underlying emotions, thoughts, and sensations.

Exercise 3.1: What Lies Beneath

In this exercise we invite you to be starkly honest. Looking closely at and authentically acknowledging what lies underneath your anger is part of changing how you relate to anger in the future.

1. Find a place to quietly explore the inner landscape of your emotions, thoughts, and sensations. Give yourself five to ten minutes to explore without interruption.

2. Read through the table of examples we've provided here. This will help you make better contact with what is happening within you as you recall times when you acted out or suppressed your anger.

3. Now choose three times when you have felt angry and either acted out or numbed it through suppression. In the table, name each with a word or a sentence, and identify whether you acted out or suppressed.

4. Close your eyes and recall each anger episode in turn, then write down the emotion, thoughts, and sensations that the anger was serving to control.

Name	Type	Emotion(s) being avoided, hidden, stifled, controlled
Example 1: Throwing the plate incident.	*Example 1:* Acting out.	*Example 1:* My feelings were hurt. I felt lonely. I had thoughts that my partner didn't care about me. I had a sinking sensation in my chest.
Example 2: Not being heard by my boss incident.	*Example 2:* Suppression	*Example 2:* Feeling humiliated and fearful, discounted. I had thoughts that I was stupid and not worth listening to. I could sense my heart beating rapidly, and I was sweating.
Example 3: Screaming at my partner and pushing her.	*Example 3:* Acting out	*Example 2:* Feeling fearful and unappreciated. I had thoughts about how she doesn't acknowledge me. If she really cared, she would do what I want. I had a sensation of tension all over my body.

1.		
2.		
3.		

5. Consider your three situations, plus any other times that have come to mind in which you have acted out or suppressed anger. Look for any common emotional themes running through them. Are there one or two emotions linked to certain thoughts and sensations that you do not want, do not like, or are unwilling to feel? For instance, are you avoiding hurt feelings more generally, or fears more generally? Are you avoiding humiliation or feeling out of control?

6. In the space provided, write about the main or more general internal experiences you would like to banish or hide by acting out or suppressing anger. Which emotions lie beneath the anger?

_____

_____

_____

Notice what you experience as you begin to acknowledge the emotions that lie beneath the anger. Notice how long you have been trying to cover them up. At this point in time, we invite you to simply notice. No action is required yet. We have more work to do before moving along, as you discover a new relationship with emotions and sensations, especially those related to anger.

Your Current Relationship with Anger and Other Emotions

Now that you're familiar with what lies beneath your anger, bringing the more vulnerable emotions into focus, we invite you to look at your relationship with these emotions—including anger.

Before we dive into this process and the next exercise, we want to acknowledge that acting out or suppressing anger are only two of the ways that people try to control unpleasant emotions. We know there are many ways to try to control what you feel, and acting out or suppressing anger is only a part of the picture. However, because you have picked up this book, it's likely that anger has hijacked you in important ways that are causing problems in your life. We suspect that other ways that you try to control emotion might be problematic as well. But we want to appeal to your experience with emotion rather than simply trust our own. By the end of this next exercise, you will get a sense of what we mean.

Exercise 3.2: Strategies for Controlling Emotions

Part I. Take time to reflect on all the different ways you try to avoid or eliminate emotion you don't like, including anger. After you have taken some time to reflect, circle each of the strategies in this table that you have been attempting, either to control anger or to escape other emotions, including anger. Write in any others that may not be listed in the Other boxes. Remember, strategies can be considered either good or bad, so circle all that apply to you.

Control Strategies

Ignoring	Prayer	Medications	Relaxation techniques
Forced calm	Alcohol	Other drugs	Avoiding eye contact
Daydreaming	Lashing out	Exercise	Planning ahead
Isolation	Ignoring my body	Joking	Sarcasm
Mumbling	Being vague	Rolling eyes	Falling silent
Not listening	Avoiding people	Zoning out	Going to bed
Working too much	Judging	Evaluating	Over/undereating
Acting out	Criticizing	Manipulating	Withdrawing
Being secretive	Changing the subject	Procrastination	Yelling
Trying to guess what others are thinking	Following rules excessively	Distraction (watching TV, social media)	Obsessing about events
Other:	Other:	Other:	Other:
Other:	Other:	Other:	Other:

Notice how each of these is either an effort to control feeling angry (suppression) or an attempt to cover other feelings with angry behavior (acting out). All can be ways to control your emotions.

Part II. With angry behavior in particular, we also try to control others as a strategy to control our emotions. Read the following statements and mark an "X" in the box next to each strategy you use to try to control your feelings by controlling others.

☐   I routinely offer unsolicited advice by pleading, persuading, or lecturing.

☐   I repeat a point over and over to get others to align their thoughts and views with mine.

☐   I communicate by telling rather than discussing.

☐   I use "should," "must," "you'd better," and similar statements when communicating.

☐   I use my anger to get my message across or force compliance by others.

☐   I use dogmatic statements, stubbornness, noncompliance, closed-mindedness, or chilling silence to influence others.

☐   I impose my choices, beliefs, and standards on others with unyielding stubbornness of conviction.

☐   I discount the behaviors, values, thoughts, opinions, and choices of others as wrongheaded and in need of my correction.

☐   I procrastinate or make only a half-hearted effort so as to get back or get even.

☐   I tend to be impatient with myself and others.

☐   I feel uneasy about loose ends and strive for closure, even if it hurts me or others.

Notice how each of these is an effort to either control feeling angry (suppression) or cover other feelings with angry behavior (acting out). Ultimately, each one of these can be ways to control your emotions.

At this point, you might be asking yourself, *What is so wrong with wanting to control my emotions?* or *Isn't it emotions that are getting me in trouble?* or *Isn't it better to be in charge of my emotions—especially if the emotions are considered negative or bad?* Well, it depends on the context and the meaning you are trying to create in life. Indeed, we know that you may have even benefited from these types of control.

Let's look at acting out on the feeling of anger itself as a form of control. When you're not controlling your angry behavior, but "discharging" it through shouting or even physical threats or violence, you may experience immediate effects that are reinforcing. This means your letting loose appears to pay off in some way; for example, by reducing stress. Not so. Discharging anger actually makes things worse in the long run.

As we discussed in the previous chapter, acting angrily *can* get others' attention. It *can* get them to stop or start doing something. Punishment or revenge may feel good in the moment. Getting others to rapidly change their behavior in response to your anger may feel powerful in the short term. Hiding your underlying emotions by being angry may feel protective and keep you from feeling vulnerable.

In the long run, however, control of underlying emotion, whether through anger or something else, is costly. The long-term payoff is tiny at best. Trying to control your true emotion creates suffering. And your life is given over to the costs of angry behavior.

Exercise 3.3: Assessing the Costs of Anger

You have probably noticed that suppressing or acting out on anger has exacted some high costs in your life. Let's dive deep into the reality of those costs and the toll that anger has taken in your life. Write about the costs or the suffering you have experienced resulting from suppressing or acting out in anger in each of the following categories. Examples might include hypertension in the area of health and loneliness in the area of relationships.

Health (examples to get you started: hypertension, heart disease, substance abuse):

_____

_____

_____

Family relationships:

_____

_____

_____

Romantic relationships:

_____

_____

_____

Friendships:

_____

_____

_____

Career:

_____

_____

_____

Spirituality:

_____

_____

_____

Personal (your feelings about yourself):

_____

_____

_____

Now review your responses, and notice that even though there might be short-term payoffs, there are always long-term costs. Reflect on how unworkable controlling emotions through anger has become. How not out of control are you? Have these control efforts led you to miss out on vital parts of your life? If your answer is yes, there is hope. Maybe control itself is the problem.

Before we move on, if you're feeling upset or bad about yourself after this exercise on costs of control, please realize that you are doing the best you can. It is essential for you to see the costs. Opening up to what is truly happening in your life is part of learning to choose more wisely. It is an important step in getting out of being trapped in a repetitive pattern of reactivity.

The Workability of Control

Many people have fallen into a trap when it comes to their emotions: the idea that emotions need to be controlled. If you look at each strategy in exercise 3.2 again, you will see the one thing they have in common: they are all attempts to reduce, eliminate, or control your emotional experience. They are designed to control anger by suppressing it or to control other emotions by using anger as a form of control.

However, the problem with these control strategies is that they don't work—at least not in the long run. They may give temporary relief, but they are too costly in terms of living well and having healthy, loving relationships, a satisfying career, and personal development. You don't need us to convince you of this problem. Simply reflect on your own experience, notice again the costs you wrote about in the preceding exercise, and check in with yourself honestly. Has control paid off for you in any significant way? If the answer is no, the good news is that there is another option. But first, let's take a closer look at how control works with feelings and thoughts.

THE PARADOX OF CONTROL

You may find that you use the same set of rules for your internal experiences (thoughts, feelings, sensations) and your external experiences (the world beyond you). The typical strategy for addressing a problem in the outer world is control. If you have a problem, find the cause and get rid of it to make the problem go away. For instance, if there's dirt on the floor, sweep it up and throw it out. If you're hungry, cook something or go out to eat. In essence, if you don't like or don't want something, figure out how to fix it, then fix it. This type of rule works in the external world. Herein lies the problem. We try to apply that same rule to internal experiences that we don't like or want.

But let's look closely. Does that rule actually work for internal experiences? For example, if you don't like what you're thinking, can you just get rid of it? If you don't like what you're feeling, can you walk away from your feelings or sensations? Can you sweep them up and throw them out? Has any attempt you have made to eliminate anger made your anger vanish? Or has venting your anger ever made other emotions permanently disappear?

What if our internal experiences—our thoughts, feelings, and body sensations—operate under a different rule? The strategies we use to apply control to the external world do not apply to our inner world. We can't control what we think or what we feel for long. In fact, trying to eliminate thoughts, feelings, and sensations through control typically creates more suffering, prolonging our existing pain and vulnerability. When we struggle with our thoughts and emotions, we add suffering to the pain that comes with being human.

One last thing about control: it's not all problematic. So letting go of control is about finding where control works and where it does not. For instance, controlling your emotions can be practical and even helpful in certain situations. The issue is excessive and misapplied control. Control itself isn't intrinsically bad; what matters is how you use it, and when. We'll explore this more in later chapters. For now, know that there are times when control of your emotions is necessary, even prudent.

TURNING CONTROL ON ITS HEAD

So, with the work in this chapter, you may find yourself confused or even shocked. You may have spent your whole life trying to control your thoughts, feelings, bodily sensations, and even other people to make things better. You may have learned from others that controlling your emotions is the answer to health and happiness. And here we have just turned that notion upside down. What do you do with the suggestion that *control* is the problem and not your anger? If trying to control anger is not the answer, then what is? Isn't this whole thing hopeless? How do you overcome the suffering in your life?

While you can't control what's inside you, you *can* control what you do with your hands, feet, and mouth. In short, the way you respond to the reality of the world is in your control. But that means showing up to yourself and your internal experience, authentically and engagingly. This can be freeing. This can be creative. This can bring hope.

It will not be easy. Letting go of controlling what you think, feel, and sense will be a challenge. However, it will give you the power to respond with choice and action.

Summary

In this chapter, we have visited all the ways in which you have become a slave to anger, by either suppressing it or acting on it. Trying to control your emotions has taken over and impacted your life. However, you are learning that the only real control we have is how we *relate* to our thoughts, feelings, and sensations, and what we do with our hands, feet, and mouth.

In the coming chapters we'll be asking you: who is in charge of you? The goal is to let go of control of your internal experiences, so they stop commanding your life. Anger no longer has to be the dictator of your behavior, your relationships, your health, and your sense of self. What would you be willing to do to get your life back? *Willingness* is the key. Let's turn to that next.

CHAPTER 4

Willingness to Experience

Life is a series of natural and spontaneous changes. Don't resist them; that only creates sorrow. Let reality be reality. Let things flow naturally forward in whatever way they like.

—Lao Tzu

Monica is a single mother of eight-year-old Jeremy. As a woman in her later thirties, she had longed to be a mom for many years but struggled to get pregnant. When she was finally able to get pregnant, Monica was both scared and excited to invite her child into the world. She was looking forward to motherhood. As a single mom, Monica felt exhausted when her child was still a baby, but she managed well most of the time.

When Jeremy turned three years old, new challenges arose. Jeremy began to throw tantrums and exhibit explosive behavior. He would hit and scream regularly. Putting him to bed each night was an Olympian task. Monica found herself becoming quite angry at her son, feeling like a victim of his behavior. Yet Monica also felt her anger was wrong. She should be grateful, she told herself, not angry. She began to punish herself for having feelings of anger—criticizing her skill as a mother and berating herself for not being able to always feel calm.

Monica pushed herself to remain in control of her emotions, trying to force feelings of gratitude. She suppressed her anger. She drank alcohol every night, took different types of pills, read every parental book available, tried to meditate the feelings away, tried to simply ignore her emotions and discount her experience—all to no avail. All the while she was still struggling. She was afraid to interact with her son, especially at night. She was scared of feeling angry and losing control. Her exhaustion and fear grew. She could see no way out of her dilemma. She felt trapped.

What Is Willingness to Experience?

Willingness is the active intention to be open to your whole experience. It is an allowing of both comfortable and uncomfortable feelings, thoughts, and sensations. It means being actively present, in each moment, to the experience of pain and joy, positive and negative thoughts, pleasant and unpleasant sensations. Willingness is allowing yourself to feel both your angry feelings and the emotions that lie beneath the anger or are hidden by it. It is about being present to your vulnerabilities without trying to make those experiences come or go.

Willingness also involves being present to the ongoing flow of your experience. As Lao Tzu put it, "Let things flow naturally forward in whatever way they like." Imagine a flowing river. There are places along the river where the water is rolling smoothly and gently flowing by. There are other places where the flow is rapid and roiling. The water is in constant motion. It is flowing. Our internal experience is much the same. Anger rises and falls, as do joy and peace. Irritation comes and goes, as do feeling loving or compassionate. Being willing is about opening your arms wide in a full stance of acceptance and letting your internal experiences flow. It is the alternative to control.

Willingness in Action

Willingness is an active state, in terms of both the stance you take toward internal experience and what you do with your feet. Let's first talk about willingness as an active state. When we open up to our internal experience and accept what we think, feel, and sense, willingness has many qualities. The stance is alive with a particular energy. Willingness in action is not giving up or giving in. It is not about resigning yourself to your feelings; rather, it is about actively opening to them, as a flower opens to the sun, each petal absorbing the rays.

Willingness to experience is a choice. You are willing, or you are not. Desiring to be willing or wanting to be willing won't get you to willing. You cannot, for instance, choose to feel only the "good" feelings and then try to control the bad. This simply won't work. Indeed, to feel good, you must be open to feeling bad. To feel joy, you must be willing to feel pain. We humans are not very good at targeting a single emotion—like anger—and controlling it. Instead, we must control them all to control one. This means if you suppress one, you suppress all.

Willingness also involves movement of the feet. That is, while taking an open stance, you also move forward in life, creating meaning. Holding what you think, feel, and sense, you step with intention toward what you care about most. Willingness is an ongoing process of holding and moving. Holding your internal experience and moving toward what you value.

Willingness in Action: Anger

It's essential to distinguish between (1) actively being present to what you feel while moving your feet and (2) being in control of your behavior. Willingness in action means feeling and behaving in ways that are consistent with your values. You can feel anger without acting on it. Willingness as an action is not about misbehaving or *acting out*. It is acting in ways that are aligned with what you want to create (a subject we'll turn to later in the book). For now, let's get you in contact with opening to feeling, thinking, sensing, *and* behaving in ways that matter.

Exercise 4.1: Opposite or Different Actions

We now invite you to review some of your past actions. Specifically, we want you to consider times when you felt one thing but did something opposite or different. These can range from minor examples to bigger ones. On the smaller side, have you ever felt a little down or apathetic, but you knew you had to go somewhere, like to an event, and so you went with your feet, even if your heart wasn't in it? Though your emotions and thoughts may have wanted you to stay home, you went anyway? This is the type of feeling/behavior contrast we are asking you to recall.

Think of times when you engaged in behavior different from what you felt like doing or what your feelings and urges seem to be telling you to do. List several specific instances where you felt one way and did the opposite or something different.

1. First recall three "general" times when you felt one way (but not angry) and did another.

    _____

    _____

    _____

2. Now recall three times when you felt anger and you did *not* suppress it or act on it.

    _____

    _____

    _____

3. Now take a few minutes and write about what you noticed by doing this exercise.

_____

_____

_____

We hope you discovered with this exercise that it is possible to feel one way and act another and that you have actually experienced this yourself. You can think, feel, and sense one thing and behave contrary to or differently from these internal experiences. You might be saying to yourself, *Yes, I can see that I can behave differently at times. But when I am furious, it just isn't possible.* We would counter that willingness to experience gives us a chance to think, feel, and sense while taking actions that are opposite or different—and, in the end, values-aligned.

Let's return to Monica's story. She felt angry at her small son Jeremy a fair bit of the time. And there were times when she imagined herself hitting Jeremy to simply get him to stop. But she never took action on these feelings and thoughts. She kept Jeremy safe. She still struggled, however. She was still unwilling. She suppressed and fought against her experience, exhausting herself. In therapy, she learned to let her feelings of helplessness and sadness be revealed. She opened up to the disappointment she felt about her experience of being a mother. She allowed herself to be angry at Jeremy. She held an open stance on her internal experience while moving her feet—taking action—in ways that helped Jeremy as well as herself.

Willingness: The Alternative to Control

Recognizing and allowing what is true inside of ourselves isn't easy. Becoming vulnerable awakens fear and thoughts about losing control. We tend to resist our so-called negative emotional experiences, fighting them to such a degree that we actually become enslaved. In chapter 3, we visited each of the ways that you have become enslaved by anger, either by engaging in behaviors to suppress it or by acting out—the costs of suppressing and acting out keep growing. For Monica, fighting against anger by suppressing it led to unhealthy behavior and emotional exhaustion. She was trapped by her own efforts to deny her experience. Turning toward what she was feeling, and the vulnerability beneath it, was her only way through her current difficulties. She just hadn't recognized this as an alternative yet.

The Battle That Didn't Need to Be Fought

When you're willing to feel your emotions, your anger, and your vulnerabilities, something remarkable happens. If you let go of the type of control you've been trying to wield, you gain a different kind of control. If you're willing to experience what goes on inside you, you can "step out" of your reactions and instead cultivate proactive responses.

Sometimes it seems like the hardest thing to do is disengage from battles that we feel we *must* fight. If you're holding on to one end of the rope in a tug-of-war, you'd better tug if you want to win! This is especially so if the pit between you and the "enemy" is a pit of despair or lost hope. If the enemy on the other side of the hole is your anger, it seems it would be better to get the anger to go into the pit rather than yourself. What if you don't win by pulling the anger into the hole? Even more impressive, what if the anger is not your enemy? What if you don't have to fight this war at all? What if the thing to do is to simply drop the rope?

The alternative to struggling with your anger and the emotions it hides is taking an open, *accepting* stance toward your thoughts, feelings, and bodily sensations. However, willingness as an alternative to control isn't the new rule. We are not saying, "You must accept." As we've noted, willingness is a choice. Would you choose to be willing if it meant your freedom? If it meant you could focus on what matters instead of on trying not to feel? We understand that it might be reasonable to not want to experience anger. It can be unpleasant. Willingness is not about wanting. Acceptance is the willingness to experience the uncomfortable sensations of anger and what is beneath it, to have access to something bigger and better for your life.

Acceptance is about experiencing anger or other emotions on their own terms. Feeling exactly what you feel when you feel it. When you're willing to experience anger or what's beneath the anger, you don't have to act out or suppress any of these experiences. This leaves you with a much more flexible set of possible actions. You might ask yourself, *What choices will I make in the presence of anger?* rather than *What choices will anger make for me?*

If you choose willingness, you are opening yourself up to a new world. It will take practice and patience. Learning to relate to your internal experience differently will not be accomplished in a day. Step by step, we'll guide you on the path to cultivating a new relationship with yourself. Let's start by looking for the truth of your experience.

Recognizing the Truth of What Is There to Feel

An important part of openness or acceptance is recognizing what is meant by this approach. There are other essential aspects of working on acceptance as well, such as simply paying attention in the moment. We'll turn to that shortly, but first, let's take a closer look at acceptance as an action.

Acceptance as an Action

As we invite you to consider acceptance as an alternative to control, we want to be clear about what is involved. Acceptance is not about accepting bad behavior. You need not accept the aggressive behavior of others or your own. Acceptance also isn't about surrender. It is not about giving up or giving in. Nor is it about being stoic—that is, being indifferent to pleasure or pain. Acceptance is about taking an active stance toward your emotional experience and choosing to adopt a particular attitude or bodily state of openness. If you were talking to yourself about it, you might say, *I am here now to feel what I feel as I feel it.* Acceptance entails an active choice with an intention to be present to whatever emotional experiences rise within—including those we call negative, such as anger or fear.

Openness to experiencing is also about noticing what your mind has to say about the experiences themselves. Our minds tend to evaluate and judge actions, sensations, and emotions. However, minds are not always accurate or helpful; indeed, their judgments can be quite painful. We'll turn more fully to your relationship with your mind in the next chapter. For now, simply note that openness to experience also involves noticing your mind without reacting to it in unhealthy or angry ways.

Simply Paying Attention

Because acceptance involves an active choice, with an intention to be present to emotional experience, then you need to learn what to pay attention to in each moment. The first step is learning to be aware of your emotional experience—simply noticing, with a gentle curiosity, what's happening with your experience as it's happening.

Of course, this journey of paying attention in the here and now can be challenging—especially when there is turmoil inside you. However, learning to pay attention, fully and without defense, can liberate you from the habits of your mind and from problematic behaviors. It can bring you into contact with the world as it truly is.

Paying attention like this also requires an ongoing commitment and a bit of courage. You will need to stick with the process of learning to observe your experiences. It takes time and practice. The benefit is that you will notice more deeply what is going on inside of you and around you. It is liberating to see the truth of your internal emotional experience. When it is time to respond, you'll have more accurate information to work with. Paying attention helps you understand yourself better, which allows you to engage with others more authentically.

You'll also need courage to make a personal commitment to grow your ability to pay attention and to follow through. There may be times when you show up to your experience and feel challenged. You might feel vulnerable or anxious. You may begin to feel angry and feel the urge to act on it. You may also get in touch with unpleasant sensations. The key here is to remember that all emotions and sensations rise and fall. Again, when you don't have to control them specifically, they can simply be an experience in the moment. You stop engaging in the tug-of-war struggle with emotions when you simply drop the rope. Remember, you're working on this because you have a purpose, a desire to change life for the better. To live by choice instead of in anger.

Finally, one of the more difficult challenges when paying attention is getting trapped in your mind. When the mind is judging you, it is easy to get hooked. When it gets caught up in stories of good and bad, right and wrong, fair and unfair, or worthy and unworthy, it can pull you away from paying attention to the landscape of your emotions and back into the desire to control by hiding and suppressing or acting out. Our minds are clever, and they constantly try to figure out who's responsible or who's to blame, who is the good one and who is the bad one. Don't be fooled. Minds are not always helpful in these situations. Noticing *that* your mind judges will be part of the experience. Be curious about this process. If you get caught by thoughts, simply acknowledge them and return to the commitment of paying attention. Remember, paying close attention to the here and now of your emotional landscape is about making your life more clear and more vital.

In the exercises that follow, we'll guide you in the practice of paying attention to your experience. We start by having you simply begin to notice sensation and the breath. This will introduce you to the process. As the exercises unfold, we invite you to look more thoroughly at more complex experiences such as emotion. Let's begin.

Exercise 4.2: A First Step in Paying Attention

The goal of this exercise is not to relax or fall asleep, but to wake up to your experience. You're going to pay attention to two specific experiences: hearing and breathing.

Begin by finding a quiet place where you can sit comfortably. You don't need to sit rigidly, but make sure your posture is upright, so you can stay alert.

First, read the full exercise so that you can complete it without having to keep opening your eyes to read. (An audio version of this exercise is available at http://www.newharbinger.com/46530. There are also materials available for download there. See the very back of this book for more details.)

Sitting upright and comfortable, gently close your eyes and simply breathe in and out for a few moments. Notice that with your eyes closed, hearing becomes more available. Turn your attention wholly to your hearing. Notice each sound that is present in the room. Notice that sound has pitch and intensity. Keep your focus on sound for a full minute or two. If you get distracted by your mind, simply refocus on sound.

After some time, shift your attention to your breathing. There is no need to change your breathing in any way; simply observe it moving in and out of your body by paying attention to it. You may notice that it is easier if you focus on a particular part of your breathing experience.

Perhaps you will notice your breath at the tip of your nostrils or the back of your throat. You may notice your chest as it rises and falls, or your belly as it inflates and deflates. Whatever feels right to you, turn your attention to that part of your breathing experience. Just as you did with hearing and sound, simply pay attention to your breathing. Follow each breath in and out for a minute or two. If you get distracted, simply acknowledge that you got distracted and return to paying attention to breathing.

After you have followed the breath for a few minutes, take a few deep breaths, open your eyes, and return to the room and your work here.

Now that you have completed the exercise, take a moment to reflect. Were you able to pay attention to sound and to breathing? Notice how, when you turn your attention to each of these in the moment, you can experience them more fully. You were aware of sound and breath. You could likely name what you heard and point to or talk about where in your body you were experiencing breathing. This is one of the benefits of paying attention: greater clarity of your experience.

When we build our capacity to pay attention, we begin to recognize what is really happening inside us and around us. As you learn to pay attention more regularly with practice, you can start to notice nuances in your experience and changes in its quality, texture, and intensity. And you can then speak to these experiences rather than merely reacting in problematic ways. Attending to what you sense and feel will help you step out of the cloudy, reactive position of being guided by control and anger.

Allowing Feelings to Be Just as They Are

As you begin to build the "paying attention muscle," you will be able to recognize what is truly happening inside of you. This will also allow you to notice any habit of resisting what is there to be felt. Reflect again on the large and small, subtle and not-so-subtle ways that you resist emotion. As we've seen, you may have been using everything from distraction to overthinking and reason-giving to acting out in ways that lead to difficulty.

If you no longer resist, allowing the feelings to be just as they are, there is less need to hide or aggress. If you accept what you feel, allowing it to be there just as it is, there is no need to control it. You can then behave in values-based ways, not driven by feelings of anger.

Paying attention to your emotional landscape is the same as paying attention to hearing or the breath. Just as you hear sounds and notice your breathing, you can do the same with emotion. As you practice paying attention to what you feel, you'll build your personal emotional knowledge. Let's practice it together.

Exercise 4.3: Allowing: Opening to Your Inner Emotional Landscape

In this exercise, we invite you to practice paying attention to whatever emotions you are feeling here and now. (An audio version of this exercise is available at http://www.newharbinger.com/46530.)

Just as you did in exercise 4.2, begin by finding a quiet place to sit comfortably. Then become aware of your emotional landscape by paying attention to what you're feeling in this moment. Take your time and begin to describe what you're feeling in detail and as fully as possible. Give your emotional experience a label. What are you noticing as you pay attention?

Take a pause. Are you sad, content, angry, anxious, or bored?

Pause again. Simply take note of whatever you're feeling right now. You might even notice a mixture of emotions. Feel free to notice and give a name to each one, taking short pauses all along as you complete the exercise. Notice whether your emotions are strong or soft. Don't block or resist the feeling, whatever it is; simply allow it as it is.

Notice the change in emotion as you continue to pay attention. Keep paying attention for several minutes. Every emotion is like a wave; it will come and go, sometimes be more intense, sometimes less. Just watch your feelings as you would watch the ocean waves, allowing them to gently roll in and out. Thoughts will inevitably come into your mind. They may be related or unrelated. No matter the thought, simply give them a brief nod or acknowledgment, saying to yourself, *there's a thought* or simply *thinking,* and choose to return your awareness to your current emotions.

As you observe your emotion, you may notice it takes up a certain amount of space in your body. You may find you can "see" this space. If so, fill it with a specific color that represents the emotion; let the color change as your emotion changes.

Remember, the point of this mindful watching is to observe what your emotion does naturally, without your intervening in any way. Just allow it to be. In this exercise, you are a curious observer, a watchful scientist, allowing your emotions to come and go simply as they rise and fall, and as they are.

After a few minutes of paying attention to your emotion, refocus your attention on this page.

Take a minute to write about what you noticed in the space provided:

_____

_____

_____

Here's an essential point: *You can do this at any time, with any emotion.* Even anger can be observed. You can watch it rise and fall like a wave on the ocean. You can observe all emotions, the ones that you avoid by being angry as well, coming into contact with them as they are in the moment. When emotions occur, you can use this type of mindful attention to observe them without getting swept off your feet; simply watch and label each feeling.

Beginning this practice—allowing emotional experience while being aware of its qualities and rise and fall—can be a turning point in making a change in your life. You no longer need to take actions linked to resisting what you feel, or act out as a means to control. You can regain your freedom to act in meaningful ways despite being angry. You can show up to what you feel instead of covering it over with anger. You will be liberated, no longer a slave to emotional control.

Again, this will take practice and patience, especially when it comes to anger. Let's try paying attention to anger specifically.

Exercise 4.4: Allowing Anger and What Lies Beneath

Prepare to write by getting paper and pen. As with the preceding exercises, find a comfortable and quiet place. (An audio version of this exercise is available at http://www.newharbinger.com/46530.)

Start by anchoring yourself with a few deep breaths.

Bring your attention to a recent situation in which your anger was a problem. Recreate the scene in your mind's eye and "walk" through the event. Try to let yourself sink into the experience as much as possible. Notice what you were seeing, hearing, and feeling at the time.

Now write down everything that you notice about your inner world during that time of anger. Allow yourself to feel the feeling as you write. Take your time. If you find yourself getting caught up in thoughts about what happened, losing the emotion, stop and take a deep breath or two. It will help you to slow down and stay focused. Remember, you are paying attention to your feelings, not your thoughts.

If it is clear to you that it is pure anger, justified and righteous, keep writing. However, if it is more than anger, if there is something beneath the anger, begin to investigate. What is being hidden? What other feelings are there to be felt? Sadness, hurt, disappointment? Let yourself be curious and explore. Write as fully as you can, contacting each of the nuances of your inner experience. Give yourself permission to simply feel as you feel, and keep writing for several minutes about the emotional experience.

Now pause and lay the pen down. Take a few deep breaths and read what you have written. Go slowly, allowing yourself to feel each emotion, whether anger or what lies beneath. Let it rise and fall, just as you did in exercise 4.3. No need to make this anger come or go; it can simply be as it is. See if you can take a stance of acceptance, opening to what you feel.

When you finish reading, take a moment to reflect on what you truly needed, based on what you have learned from paying attention to your experience concerning this incident of anger. If the emotional experience could speak about your vulnerabilities, what would it say? Instead of what the forceful behavior and hiding would seem to demand, what would this vulnerability truly want? Write your response in the space provided.

_____

_____

_____

Finally, take the piece of paper you wrote on and place it where you'll see it. Of course, keep it private if you need to. Just as the paper's landscape holds the written words of your story and makes no effort to erase the words or crumple to hide itself, let your body be the landscape that holds the feelings of your life. Use the paper to remind yourself as often as you need.

Allowing yourself to experience emotion, as noted, will take practice. A single exercise or two will not suffice to make a change. You can practice and expand all of these exercises. We recommend that you keep regularly engaging in practices like these. You might take up mindfulness meditation to grow your experience with paying attention, thus increasing your knowledge of yourself and your clarity around your experience. This is an essential part of overcoming angry behavior and suppression of other emotions.

Summary

When Monica completed exercise 4.4, she had tears in her eyes. She had realized that beneath her anger she really needed to be seen and cared about by others. This was a true revelation to her. In that moment, she realized that suppressing her anger had only made things worse. She also discovered that she had real needs. Instead of fighting with her anger, she opened up to it. Willingly and with an intentional stance of openness to emotion, she began to let herself feel. In this space she was able to engage in self-care.

Allowing your anger and your vulnerable emotions is a first step in letting go of the need to suppress or act out. It is the first step in making change. By dropping the tug-of-war rope, letting go of control of your internal experience, you make space for something new to happen. When you no longer need to control your emotion by suppressing or acting out, you're free to manage your behaviors. You are free to choose instead of the emotions choosing for you.

There is more work to do, however. We know this is a journey, and more skills and practice will be needed. Onward!

CHAPTER 5

Recognizing Mind

Develop a mind that is vast like space, where experiences both pleasant and unpleasant can appear and disappear without conflict, struggle or harm. Rest in a mind like a vast sky.

—Majjhima Nikāya

Alex is nearly seventy. He describes himself as a "self-made" man. He has grown his business over the years and is now quite wealthy. He likes feeling powerful, and he is known by others as strong.

Despite these successes, everyone is frightened of him, especially his wife, Maria. Maria feels ashamed of Alex and his ability to intimidate others with his anger. When he is angry, he shouts and turns red in the face. His outbursts are characteristically loud, and his body language is animated. Maria must regularly try to calm him down or work to not make him angry. She is afraid to go out to dinner with Alex, because if something is wrong with the food or service, he starts a massive quarrel with the staff and begins insulting the restaurant. When they go out with friends, everyone knows that nobody should contradict Alex. If they do, he starts shouting and reiterating his opinion.

Alex is stuck in believing that he is always right. In his view, others simply don't understand, aren't as smart as him, or can't articulate accurately. The rest of the world is wrong, and he lets others know his opinion.

Alex is fused with what his mind has to offer. He cannot see things differently. This type of inflexibility is costing Alex. His wife and others are fed up with his behavior. His angry explosions are leading those close to him to avoid him. Alex is experiencing ever-growing loneliness.

You and Your Mind

Alex has a very human problem. He is fused with his mind. That is, Alex thinks of himself and his mind as the same thing. There is no distinction between Alex and his thoughts. What if, however, Alex is a human being *with* a mind instead of a human being who *is* a mind. What if Alex could observe his thinking? If he were able to be aware of his thoughts in a nonattached fashion, Alex might behave differently. Instead of reflexively reacting to thoughts about how "right" he is, he could observe his thoughts. This unattached perspective—*I have a mind; I am not a mind*—might help Alex be less reactive, calm his boisterous behavior, and preserve his relationships.

This chapter will help you learn how to relate more wisely to your mind and your thoughts. The overall goal is to free you from having a mind that dictates how you behave to living a life guided by your values. Defusion, and the acceptance we explored in chapter 4, will work together to help you create a meaningful life.

What Is Fusion with the Mind?

Let's explore what it means to be fused with your mind. Fusion is a process by which two or more things are brought together to make a single entity. Think of mixing flour, sugar, butter, and eggs. If you blend all of these together, they become fused into a sweet batter. The single items no longer exist. This is a good metaphor for what can happen to us and our minds. When we start to learn how to talk as small children, the "mixing" begins. We forget that we were once separate ingredients—a child with no words, and the words themselves.

We hope you find it interesting to note this distinction, and we'll explore fusion more fully in a minute. At this point, we want to introduce you to *defusion*, or a way to remember the separate ingredients.

What Is Defusion from the Mind?

Defusion from the mind is the skill of learning to see thoughts for what they are—thoughts. Learning to do this can help you when you're feeling stuck inside of thoughts related to anger. If you can see the separate ingredients in the moment—you and your thoughts—you can learn to respond to those thoughts in different ways. Rather than responding as if you and your thoughts are the same thing, you can respond in ways that are more workable concerning your values and what is needed in the moment.

Defusion can also help you see the ongoing flow of thinking. Thinking is a continuous process. We are always thinking or having thoughts. There's you, and there's your ongoing thinking. This is important, because it can remind you that thoughts will come and go, rise and fall. When you're feeling angry, you can seem to get stuck in thoughts, ruminating (a subject we'll turn to shortly) about what has caused the anger. In this place, you get caught up in thinking, completely losing the separate ingredients. They have become fused.

Now it may seem as if you are powerless to your thoughts. They are the dictators of your behavior. But if in those moments you can defuse, you'll regain your power to behave in more workable ways.

With defusion, we'll help you learn to once again separate the ingredients—you and your mind. In this separation you have the space to choose; your mind is no longer the dictator of what you do. If you are separate from your mind, you can make choices apart from what it is demanding in the moment. This is a very effective way to change behavior concerning anger. When you have angry thoughts, you can step back, see them for what they are, and notice that thoughts flow. The angry thoughts will pass.

Before we move on to different types of defusion exercises, let's learn a little about fusion and its antidote. This will help you understand how fusion begins to form and to see that you are not alone, nor are you to blame. We all learn to think, and we all fuse with our thinking.

Fusion and Defusion: Evaluation, Construction, and Rumination

As we learned to talk as small children, as we learned more words, we learned how to relate those words together so the mind began to develop and we began to think. As time went on, we became fully thinking beings. We each developed a mind. And as our mind grew with knowledge, along with its ever-present commentary, just as the sugar and eggs come together when beaten, the distinction between the person with a mind and the mind itself gets lost. That is, we and our minds get mixed. We become fused with our minds.

One critical problem with fusion with the mind is that we lose perspective. We get entangled with what our mind is saying and begin to view the world from this fused place. It is like looking at the world with a red bubble over your head. Everything looks red from inside that bubble. The red view can color how we see ourselves and the world. It can make us think we know things we don't actually know.

Let's return to Alex. It couldn't possibly be that Alex is always right. Indeed, we feel pretty sure, as do Maria and her friends, that Alex is sometimes wrong, maybe even a lot. Minds, although quite valuable and useful, can get us into trouble. When we cling too tightly to what our mind has to say, when we live from inside the bubble only, we become inflexible. This is what has happened to Alex. Let's take a closer look.

You have probably at some time in your life heard someone claim the moon is made of cheese. We suspect that you don't believe this claim, no matter how many times you have heard it, even though the crater-pocked moon can look like Swiss cheese. Clearly, not all claims are believable or true. So perhaps for this moment, we can at least acknowledge that minds don't know everything—even if they have the thought the moon is made of cheese. You don't need to believe what your mind says all the time, even if your mind says it is true.

Now let's look at a different type of thought. Have you ever thought you were really right about something and then later learned that you were not? If you answered yes, don't worry. We have all had that happen from time to time. Minds can be very sure of what they think. Perhaps, then, you can begin to see how if you fuse with your mind, trouble can emerge. You might act on something your mind says without taking the opportunity to notice other perspectives. *The world is red, and there are no other colors.* You get locked in, and flexibility disappears. Red begins to dictate how you behave. In Alex's case, if red equals right, then conflict will follow him wherever he goes.

If we draw this example out just a bit more, the trouble becomes clearer. Alex has the thought that *Waiters should always get my order right.* There are at least two problems when he fuses with this thought. First, everyone makes mistakes, and second, why should waiters always have to get it right? Whose rule is that? When Alex is fused with this thought when he is out to eat, there is no room for error. Going out to eat becomes an anxious, unpleasant event, rather than a warm, relaxing night out.

We do not want to give the impression that minds are not useful. They certainly are. Minds help us plan, organize, predict, tell stories, remember, and stay safe, among many other things. There is much to appreciate about our minds. We are not too worried about minds when they are helping us. But minds also evaluate, construct, and ruminate in ways that are not useful. Let's look at each to see what it is that we mean.

Minds Evaluate

As our minds develop, we learn how to evaluate things as good or bad. We learn how to evaluate by many measures—beautiful or ugly, dangerous or safe, and so on. However, we don't learn that the goodness and the badness do not exist in the objects being evaluated. To our evaluating minds, it seems the object itself is good or bad. We forget the distinction between what we say about objects and the object itself. For instance, if we ask you to evaluate whether a movie you saw was good or bad, you likely could do it, but the goodness or badness of the film doesn't exist in the movie itself. Indeed, the same movie that you evaluate as bad, someone else could evaluate as good. We evaluate persons, places, things, activities—but our evaluation exists not within those items, but apart from them. Recognizing this can help. If you've been evaluating the behavior of other people or situations in ways that make you feel distressed and angry—and then you recognize that your evaluation is just that, *your evaluation* and nothing more—you might make a different choice. Instead of suppressing or acting out on this anger, you can defuse (seeing the red bubble for what it is) and choose to behave in a values-based way.

Exercise 5.1: Noticing How Your Mind Evaluates

In this exercise, we invite you to notice evaluation in two different arenas. The first is simply general evaluation and recognizing how we can evaluate nearly anything. The second is evaluation concerning anger. (A downloadable file is available at http://www.newharbinger.com/46530.)

Starting with general evaluation, begin to look around the room you're sitting in and select five objects. Write the name of those objects in the first column of this table. Now return to the objects one by one and begin to evaluate each. Is the object good or bad? Feel free to use other evaluations like *beautiful* or *ugly, pleasant* or *unpleasant,* and so on. Write your evaluation in the second column. In the third column, write a reason why you made that evaluation. We provide an example to give you the basic idea.

	Object	Evaluation	Reason
Ex.	Light bulb	Bad	It is not bright enough for my needs.
1.			
2.			
3.			
4.			
5.			

Now go through the list of five objects a second time. This time give the objects the opposite evaluation and a reason for why you gave that evaluation.

	Object	Evaluation	Reason
Ex.	Light bulb	Good	I can see well enough to get the things I need.
1.			
2.			
3.			
4.			
5.			

We hope you discover that any object can be evaluated, and that the evaluation is not in the object itself. You are doing the evaluating and can give a perfectly good reason for why you evaluated the object that way. You can also change your evaluation and provide a perfectly good reason for why you evaluated it oppositely. Evaluation doesn't exist in what is being evaluated; rather, it is something that minds can do...and so they do.

Now let's turn to the second task in this exercise. Again, we invite you to look at the way your mind evaluates, this time concerning anger. In the first column, write about three different instances of anger in which you suppressed or acted out. Consider what evaluations your mind was making at the time. Was it evaluating a person or situation or both? Note the evaluation and the thing your mind was evaluating in the second column. In the third column, rate how stuck you were in those evaluations, on a scale of 1 to 10, with 1 being not at all stuck and 10 being completely stuck—feeling unable to change or free yourself from the evaluation.

	Anger instances	Situation or person being evaluated and evaluation	Reason for evaluation	Rating (1 to 10)
Ex.	Sally made fun of me at Wes's party.	I evaluate Sally as stupid.	She is stupid because she cannot recognize when she is not being funny.	9
1.				
2.				
3.				

Now go through your three instances of anger a second time. This time give the situation or person the opposite evaluation and a reason why you gave that evaluation. Rate how stuck you might be if this second evaluation were the case, but it was in addition to the evaluation you gave above, so both evaluations were present at the same time. It doesn't have to be a lower number. But check and see if changing perspective helps.

	Anger instances	Situation or person being evaluated and evaluation	Reason for evaluation	Rating (1 to 10)
Ex.	Sally made fun of me at Wes's party.	I evaluate Sally as smart.	It was amusing the way she made that joke about me.	6
1.				
2.				
3.				

Notice here, too, that the evaluation doesn't exist in the person or situation. If you can see your mind's evaluations—and even get it to do the opposite evaluation—you're helping yourself become more flexible, especially when responding to anger.

In this exercise we hope you can see that minds can evaluate anything at any time. We also hope that by trying on different evaluations of the same thing or the same event, you gain a little perspective on evaluation. Even if you only defuse from it briefly, sometimes that is all you need to choose a different behavior, even when you feel anger.

Minds Construct

Because we can imagine with our minds, we can imagine the future. This can be helpful when we need to plan for something that is coming along. However, it can also lead to difficulty if an imagined future makes you feel fearful, anxious, righteous, or angry. You can act on these feelings in ways that lead to problems. You can likely remember a time when you were imagining something terrible that brought up feelings of anger. For instance, suppose you think a coworker is competing with you. As you consider this issue, you begin to picture her doing things in the future that include shutting you out. As you continue to imagine the different scenarios of competition, you grow angrier and angrier.

Here your mind may not be your friend. It is helpful to remember that the future has not arrived yet, even though your mind has imagined that it has. We do not know what the future holds. It is better to be patient and see what happens than to react in anger to an imagined future and, even worse, eventually realize that constructed future did not actually unfold.

Exercise 5.2: Noticing How Your Mind Constructs

With this exercise we ask you to notice how minds can't actually predict what will happen. It is a good distinction to carry with you as you move forward in life.

You are invited to write about two ways of looking at how the mind constructs: one from your past and one that you find yourself thinking about now.

Begin with the experience from your past. Think of a time when you thought that something, for sure, was going to unfold in a particular way—and then it didn't. Spend some time reflecting on that experience before you write.

Now write about your mind's construction back then, paying close attention to what your mind imagined and what actually happened. Be honest with yourself. Notice the distinction between your mind's construction and the reality of the event. Notice the places where your mind got it wrong or was inaccurate.

_____

_____

_____

_____

_____

Now think about something that makes you angry now. As you reflect on this, notice what your mind is saying about it in terms of the future. What is your mind constructing? Write about it here.

_____

_____

_____

_____

_____

Now take that same anger-provoking event and construct a completely different future from the one you just wrote about. Write about it here.

_____

_____

_____

_____

We could ask you to do another writing exercise, taking the same event and constructing yet another completely different future from the two above. Feel free to try this out if you like. Minds are good at this and can create all kinds of future outcomes. More important, notice that your mind constructs.

Now defuse from those constructions, at least enough to not get entangled in such fashion as to lose your values to angry behavior.

In the preceding exercise we invited you to look at how the mind constructs futures. The main point is to notice the constructing. Minds imagine all kinds of future outcomes. The problem is that what is constructed is rarely what actually happens. This is true even if your mind says, *Yeah, but it was close to what I constructed in my mind.* You cannot know the future, no matter how imaginative your mind may be. Holding your mind's constructions lightly, viewing them for what they are—constructions—can help you make choices based on values instead of just your mind's constructions.

Minds Ruminate

Minds are very good at going over a thought, a scene, or an incident again and again, especially when something is emotionally challenging or related to something that makes you angry. We can find a less charged example quite easily. How often have you heard the words to a song only to find that you can't get it out of your head? The song or a line from the song repeats over and again. It is hard to shake the words out. They just seem to finally wear away after you get focused on other things. Something like a song getting stuck in your head is relatively common (there's even a term for it: *ear worm*). Minds are good at looping around and around.

This happens not only with songs, but also with other thoughts. For some people this is really challenging, even debilitating. They struggle so much with the looping of specific thoughts that they can get diagnosed with obsessive-compulsive disorder (OCD). You may have heard of this before.

People have stressful thoughts: *I left the stove on* or *I forgot to lock the door*—or, even worse, that they might harm someone they love.

The bigger problem with OCD is that people with this disorder often compulsively respond to those thoughts. They might check the stove a hundred times a day to make sure it is turned off. They might get stuck performing a task such as rhythmically locking the door ten times and counting out loud with each turn of the lock. They may feel compelled to perform rituals like making sure they never step on a crack, as it truly might break their mother's back. In this latter example, it's a superstition that is playfully indulged in by children. But for those with OCD, the compulsion is severe, and the rituals overtake their lives.

This is relevant to anger in several ways. First, your mind can get stuck on an incident where you had feelings of anger, and what you did in response to that incident. The issue plays over and over again in your head. You are ruminating about what happened, what could happen, and what brought about the anger. The story of the anger just doesn't seem to stop rolling through your mind.

If you observe your thinking, you will discover that these thoughts might roll through for a bit, but then your mind is occupied with other things. Yes, of course, the thoughts related to anger can return. Remember, thoughts rise and fall. And just as the person with OCD learns to not act on their thoughts, instead seeing them for what they are, we invite you to do the same using defusion techniques. But first, a final exercise looking at fusion in the area of rumination.

Exercise 5.3: Noticing How Your Mind Ruminates

In this exercise, we use a scale linked to rumination about anger.

Think of an incident of anger, and in the space provided, write a summary sentence about it. Then write a specific thought related to that incident. This thought can be anything from how it turned it out to an evaluation about another person. Just make sure it is a *single thought* about you or what happened during the angry incident.

Now, on the first scale, place an X for the amount of time you spent ruminating on that angry incident. On the second scale, place an X for the number of times the thought related to that anger incident rolled through your mind. This doesn't have to be exact. We recognize that it is difficult to time rumination and count thoughts, but do your best to mark an X wherever it feels right to indicate the magnitude of your rumination on the issue.

First incident: _____

Thought related to the incident: _____

0 = No time spent thinking about it

10 = A lot of time spent thinking about it

0 ——————————————————————————————————————> 10

0 = Thought passed through my head only a few times

10 = Thought passed through my mind a good many times

0 ——————————————————————————————————————> 10

Now think of another incident, and follow the same directions.

Second incident: _____

Thought related to the incident: _____

0 = No time spent thinking about it

10 = A lot of time spent thinking about it

0 ——————————————————————————————————————> 10

0 = Thought passed through my head only a few times

10 = Thought passed through my mind a good many times

0 ——————————————————————————————————————> 10

Now answer the following questions:

1. Did the time you spent on the specific thought and the number of times it went through your mind change what happened in any significant way? If yes, how so?

    _____

    _____

2. Did the time spent on the specific thought and the number of times it went through your mind create any frustration for you? If yes, how so?

    _____

    _____

3. Did you wish you could stop thinking about it? And did the wish come true when you needed it to?

    _____

    _____

If you're like most people, when it comes to ruminating about anger, the rumination did not change the outcome in any significant way, nor how few or many times the thought passed through your mind or how much time you spent on the thought. Minds ruminate. Given this, defusion is your ally. One effective approach to the never-ending commentary of the mind is to gently observe the ongoing flow of thinking without getting caught up in the thoughts.

Changing the Relationship with Thoughts and Thinking

When people experience thoughts they don't like, they tend to try to get rid of them. They begin to think that their mind isn't working correctly and needs to be fixed. Now you might think to yourself, *I get it. The way to not get angry is to make sure I don't have angry thoughts or thoughts related to anger.* But remember what you learned in chapter 4: The more you try not to think a thought, the more you think it. The alternative, as noted, is to defuse.

Ways to Defuse from Thoughts

We now present three quick strategies to help you defuse from thoughts; these may be helpful in overcoming either acting on or suppressing anger.

Labeling Thoughts

First strategy: Practice labeling your thoughts. You can describe your thoughts as something your *mind* is doing rather than something *you* are doing. For example, you can say to yourself, *I'm having the thought that I can't stand my anger, I have to do something.* And, you can take it one step further and say to yourself, *I notice that I'm having the thought that I can't stand my anger.* If you think, like Alex, that someone else is wrong, you would say, *I'm having the thought that Maria is wrong.* Taking it one step further, you would say, *I notice that I'm having the thought that Maria is wrong.*

Give it a try. In the space provided, fill in the blanks with thoughts you have related to anger.

I'm having the thought that _____

I notice that I'm having the thought that _____

I'm having the thought that _____

I notice that I'm having the thought that _____

Practice this strategy with all thoughts, but especially with thoughts you are fused with related to anger. The more you practice, the more you will notice that thoughts are something you have and can notice, rather than thoughts being something you literally are.

Find Your Mind's Typical Sound Tone or Tune

Second strategy: Check to see if your mind seems to make a particular kind of sound tone or tune when it is angry or having sticky, fused thoughts. For instance, you may notice that your mind's sound tone or tune is "gruff" when you are angry, or higher in pitch (like it is almost yelling). Once you recognize the tone, begin to sing or repeat it whenever you notice that your mind is fusing with evaluating or other anger-related thoughts. You can sing, "My mind is being gruff and it is saying _____" (fill in the blank with the words your mind is saying), or you can repeat what it is saying, exaggerating the gruffness. Be sure to repeat it multiple times. The idea is to get defused by being playful, not to fuse more tightly. This can be particularly helpful when your mind is ruminating. Give it a try now. If it feels silly, no worries; this means defusion is likely happening.

Treating Mind as a Separate Person

Third strategy: You can give your mind a name and take your mind's opinion into account, just like you would a friend's. What does "Carmen" or "Jerry" have to say about your anger? Imagine that Carmen or Jerry likes to give you opinions and advice. But remember, you are your own person. You can listen, but with the aid of defusion, you also don't have to believe or follow the opinions and advice.

The Power of Defusion

The path to relating more wisely to your mind, especially when you're angry, can be challenging. Sometimes, with anger, you can get entirely stuck inside the thoughts in your mind, almost like you're in a trance. The thoughts dictate your behavior and sometimes are so blinding that you can't see the suffering it brings to you and to others. If you find that defusing from your thoughts gets tricky, don't worry; this effort is only about practicing. Be patient with yourself. It may take time, but you're headed toward the goal of gaining your freedom. Defusion will provide the essential space in which you will be able to choose.

Thoughts can be a powerful phenomenon in your life, and they have even more power when you remain fused with them and they push you around. You regain your power when you defuse: seeing angry thoughts, and thoughts in general, for what they are—thoughts. When you can observe the ongoing flow of thinking, you free yourself from the mind as dictator, giving yourself flexibility.

Exercise 5.4: Looking at Thought Streams

Begin this exercise by sitting in a quiet place where you can practice observing your thoughts. Read through the full script first and then engage in the awareness practice. If you need to, you can refer back to the instructions. (An audio version of this exercise is available at http://www.newharbinger.com/46530.)

Start by taking a few deep breaths, allowing yourself to settle into the moment. Then bring your attention to thinking. Notice if a single thought seems to arise or thoughts seem to be coming and going. Be aware of each thought, as much as possible, as it comes into your mind. As soon as you become aware of a fully formed thought, make a mental note: *thinking*. Whisper the word *thinking* softly in your mind. Then wait for another thought to arise or form and again label it softly, saying to yourself: *thinking*.

Notice as you engage in the observation of thinking that sometimes thoughts are quick little fragments, others loud and fully formed. Sometimes they seem to be like trains barreling through your mind. Sometimes they are like soft petals loosened from the flower, floating to the ground. Don't try to analyze or hold onto them. Don't believe or disbelieve, just acknowledge thinking. Also, see if you can tune your "radar" to become aware of the type of thought that appears. Is it a judgmental thought? Does it seem heavy or light? Is it loud or soft? What is the tone of the thought? Is it soft or loud? Notice the qualities of your mind's thinking as you continue to let thoughts gently pass.

The key to this exercise is to notice thoughts rather than getting caught up in them. See if you can detect the difference between being inside the thought stream (fusion) and being outside the thought stream (defusion). Keep watching thoughts for several minutes. If you find yourself interacting with your thoughts, simply notice that and bring yourself back to the stance of observing thinking. As you observe thoughts and the ongoing flow of thinking, remember, each thought does not require you to act; thinking doesn't make you do anything, and it doesn't mean anything about you. You are a person with a mind, you are not the mind itself. Observing a stream doesn't make you the stream.

Practicing mindfulness, or nonjudgmentally observing your thoughts, can help with defusion. Consider a mindfulness practice of your own that includes gently observing the ongoing flow of thoughts.

Anger-Fueling Thoughts

As noted, minds can evaluate everything around us. This can be helpful. It assists us in looking out for danger, for instance. Evaluative minds can help us look for food, shelter, and safety by evaluating our circumstances. This essential process happens very quickly. So quickly, in fact, that we don't even notice the evaluations most of the time. Most of the time this is okay. However, when we are angry it can cause real problems.

There are certain types of evaluative thoughts that tend to fuel angry feelings. Many people report that, when they are angry, they barely recognize that they are thinking. Angry thoughts seem particularly sticky, with fusion happening in less than an instant. These thoughts also tend to have a certain flavor. Let's take a look at your sticky thoughts in this area and see if any themes emerge.

Exercise 5.5: Acknowledging Thoughts That Fuel Anger

We invite you to keep a diary during the next week. In the diary, write about each time you become angry, noting whether you act out or suppress the anger. At the end of the week, answer the following questions:

1. What did you believe, in those moments of anger? What were the key thoughts?

    _____

    _____

2. Were there typical thoughts or thoughts that you recognize as occurring across situations of anger?

    _____

    _____

3.   What were the themes? Were these being repeated, running through your mind again and again?

_____

_____

Now reflect on the themes you noticed, and consider whether they are similar in any way to these:

• You've been *harmed* (victimized) *deliberately*.

• The other person is *wrong* (unfair) and should have behaved differently.

First, know that you are not alone. These themes are often present in anger. Even if you're right, notice how these themes can fuel anger. If the goal is to stop pouring gas on the fire, defusing from thoughts that fuel anger will be crucial.

Anger-Fueling Thoughts: The Shoulds and Musts

The mind regularly judges other people and will often assess their behavior as right or wrong. Your mind can also judge your behavior as right or wrong. With judgment, your mind may be seeming to state an indisputable fact about something or someone. When this happens, you may mistakenly believe that something needs to be done. You might demand or command, either silently or out loud, that people are to act in particular ways. You might find yourself having thoughts about how someone *should* or *must* do something. You might find yourself thinking that they *have to* and *ought to*. Herein lies the problem. Others are just as free as you are, and accordingly, they do not *have* to do anything just because you think they should. The conflict begins, and anger can participate fully.

Let's return to Alex. Alex was always judging people's behavior. They were wrong, and he was right. With this fusion in place, he felt entitled. He often said to others, "That's not the right way to do it; you should do it my way." Alex created loneliness by insisting, which was fueled by being fused with his thoughts, holding them to be literally true. With the practices of defusion, Alex was able to loosen the grip his mind had on him and begin interacting with others in ways that were more acceptable and freer.

Anger-Fueling Thoughts: Causes of Behavior, Not!

We like to understand cause and effect. It makes life a bit more predictable. We put our minds to seeking answers to clarify and explain our own behavior and the behavior of others. The mind goes to work, finding the underlying causes of events, continually asking *Why?* Although there is nothing inherently wrong with wanting to know why something has happened, when it comes to anger, the need to understand cause and effect can lead to three big problems.

First, if we don't know why something has happened, we might try to guess others' intentions, feelings, and motives. In effect, we're trying to read their minds. Unfortunately, these guesses are often inaccurate. Anger can be about something that is based on a false assumption. This can create needless suffering. Defusion from assumptions can be useful to alleviate such suffering.

Second, we may blame others for our emotional pain. When we are in pain, it makes sense to seek the cause. Often understanding *why* the pain is happening can seem to help relieve it. However, blaming others leads to more significant problems. It can be quite difficult to admit that we play a role in our own pain or that we don't have control over something that has caused us pain. So our minds start playing the blame game, both passively and aggressively. Defusion from blame is the antidote.

Third, we can get lost in reasons. We come up with reasons to justify our actions: "I hit the wall because you made me angry." "I shouted at you because you do stupid things." These habits of our minds cause a lot of problems. Reasons, no matter how good they may be, do not cause behavior. Thoughts about anger or being angry do not cause people to hit walls, and having thoughts that others are stupid does not cause us to shout. Indeed, no thought causes a behavior, but fusion makes it look like it does. Again, defusion is the solution.

Summary

When you are fused with your thoughts, it is challenging to be flexible. The very fusion itself pulls you away from choice and the capacity to see alternatives. Practicing defusion will be a significant part of learning how to have anger-related thoughts without suppressing them or acting on them. We encourage you to regularly practice the exercises in this chapter. Mindfulness practice will be particularly helpful. Observe your thoughts as thoughts; notice the continuous flow of thinking. These practices can become your faithful ally in overcoming the problematic behavior you experience related to anger. As we continue, defusion will continue to be essential and helpful to other skills you learn in this workbook about how to manage your anger. We'll now turn to the next skill: perspective taking, or contacting a larger sense of self.

CHAPTER 6

Who Am I?
Contacting a Larger Sense of Self

We waste so much energy trying to cover up who we are when beneath every attitude is the want to be loved, and beneath every anger is a wound to be healed, and beneath every sadness is the fear that there will not be enough time.

—Mark Nepo, *The Book of Awakening*

Ben and his wife, Lydia, first sought couples counseling at Ben's request. He had never wanted to go to therapy. Still, he ultimately felt there was no other way to deal with what was happening to his marriage. Ben had always been "hotheaded," but he found himself more impatient as the years went on. At the same time, his wife was becoming less tolerant of his behavior, feeling ever more annoyed at his seeming inability to handle things calmly. Ben knew that his relationship with his wife was becoming more distant, a result of the seriousness of the growing problems from his anger outbursts. When his wife confronted him in the therapy sessions, he would say, "I'm like this. I'm temperamental. I can't change. Get over it or leave."

Lisa came to therapy to get help with anxiety. She would get angry with herself for feeling anxious in a crowd or not speaking up about her needs. She explained to her therapist that she would become quite annoyed with herself and didn't understand her own behavior. She could see no need to feel anxious, yet she did. Lisa described herself as a "good girl," not one to make waves or make others feel uncomfortable. She always spoke softly and waited, noticing her anxiety when she wanted to talk more or take the lead. Time and time again, she would leave social situations and become angry with herself for feeling anxiety. She reflected that it seemed unfair for such a good girl to suffer the way she did.

Confusing Description of the Self with the Self

These two short client descriptions are good examples of *confusing descriptions of the self with the self.* In chapter 5, we learned about how the mind develops through language, and how once it takes off, it can do all kinds of things. It can, for example, evaluate, construct, and ruminate. Each is a separate way that the mind does its work. As a part of that process, minds also create identities or coherent stories about who we seem to be. With anger, those stories can be about past behavior and regrets. They can be about the need to control.

Let's grow our understanding of this issue by looking at someone who's a newscaster. Let's imagine that it is Lisa. As a newscaster, Lisa may describe herself as someone who can summarize and deliver incoming information quite well. She may also say, "I am a news consumer," noting how important it is to digest the news. She may say that she is a journalist always working on new material to present on television. She may also view herself as a figurehead of wisdom and truth, and willing to take risks in the field to scoop the next story. Lisa is a newscaster.

Each of these descriptions of Lisa may be entirely true. We wouldn't argue with Lisa's descriptions, necessarily. However, we would argue that Lisa is much more than a newscaster, even if she sees this aspect of herself as her key identity. Lisa also happens to be a daughter, a mother, a sister, a community member, a wife, and an excellent bridge player, to name a few of the other roles in her life. You could say that Lisa has many identities. She plays many roles in her life, including one called a newscaster.

Lisa's describing herself as a newscaster isn't problematic unless she lives as *only* a newscaster. Let's imagine that Lisa becomes so identified with herself as a newscaster that she loses all other roles. It might start to cause difficulties in her relationships. She might begin to report the news to her husband, family, and community members. When she gets invited to parties, she might find herself letting others know that she is a newscaster and spends her time talking about the news. She may argue with others about what is wise and true, and constantly belittle those who don't pay that much attention to the news.

You can see the problem, right?

In this scenario, Lisa has become overidentified with one aspect of herself. She has forgotten to be a daughter, a sister, a wife, a community member, and so on. In this scenario, she has lost her capacity to step in and out of the different roles she has in life. This may reduce her flexibility, making her less adaptable to changing situations. Thus Lisa may become rigid in her behavior, unwilling to hear feedback or make a change. If a situation calls on her to do something other than being steeped in the news, she may find it difficult.

Lisa is not alone. In chapter 5, we noted how hard it can be to escape from the mind's red bubble. We each have a multitude of identities, and some of us get stuck in certain ones, or in certain parts of an identity. For example, if Lisa really believes that newscasters are always "wise and true," she may get stuck in believing herself to be that way, ignoring the parts of herself that might indicate otherwise. If others test her overidentification with this aspect of herself, she may become angry, being inflexible and unable to respond from other aspects of herself, her view narrowed and her capacity to take different perspectives limited.

Return to Ben and Lisa at the beginning of the chapter and reread the opening paragraphs. You can see that each has fallen into the trap of overidentification with an identity or a description of the self. Ben has fallen into the identity of "I'm temperamental," and Lisa has fallen into the identity of "good girl." Both descriptions of Ben and Lisa are, in part, accurate. However, overall they are not even close to accurate. We tend to get so used to these stories about ourselves that they become automatic, like a habit. We buy them, believing that there are no other possibilities or ways to move. We become the descriptions we have about ourselves rather than a larger self who can create those descriptions. This type of self-limitation can set us up for confrontation and other problems if we don't acknowledge them and act on them more flexibly, especially if anger is part of the story.

The Trouble with Relying on Description Alone

The difficulty with attachment to these descriptions or broader stories about ourself is twofold. First, as you'll recall from chapter 5, the words we use to describe ourselves do not exist inside us. For example, the word *newscaster* doesn't live inside Lisa; she does not have to fuse with that word. It is a word she uses to describe the aspect of her that identifies her profession. Similarly, the descriptions *I'm temperamental* and *I'm a good girl* do not exist inside Ben and Lisa, respectively. These, too, are words they use to describe an aspect of themselves—words they can defuse from. Remember, the thing described and the description are two separate things. This is a topic we'll explore more broadly shortly.

Second, attachment to these descriptions limits behavior change. The more attached you are to a description of yourself, the more it seems that you can't change. You can get a sense of this with the example of Ben. Indeed, he even refers to his inability to change, declaring to his wife, "This is me; get over it or leave." Not only does this make it difficult for his wife, but it also entirely limits Ben. If he buys the description that he *is temperamental,* it seems nothing can be done. Live with his anger or go away. This may feel quite bad for Ben's wife, but it is also incredibly disempowering for Ben. If he chooses to make change while in therapy, his attachment to his story—being a victim of his temperament—may paralyze his possibilities. And Lisa? She is at the mercy of being the good girl; she is powerless to take a stance. Both Ben and Lisa would benefit from becoming aware of a sense of self that is more than any single identity.

In this chapter, we hope to free you from the overattachment to descriptions of yourself that limit your freedom and seem to keep you from making behavior change. We have been exploring throughout the book diverse ways for you to be with your anger. We are optimistic that this work has started to help you change how you relate to anger. Still, we recognize that more is needed. As you realize that the thing described and the description are two separate things, you can begin to form a new and different relationship to your anger.

Sometimes, the more significant obstacle to change is that we get entrenched in our descriptions, identities, and behaviors tied up with those identities. We keep engaging in those behaviors, believing that is *who we are.* Beginning the process of becoming aware of how we buy into these descriptions, and how we get fused with an identity, can be quite challenging and make us feel quite vulnerable. It means taking an honest look at how we describe ourselves and how we cling to those descriptions in unhealthy ways. Doing this work can also be immensely powerful. Being aware first and then defusing from these stories of yourself is part of connecting to a much broader sense of you—a sense of you that is free to choose behaviors different from the description. Let's first look at the attachments to identities—something we call *the small self.*

Exercise 6.1: Identifying the Small Selves That Keep You Stuck

Begin by recalling several situations in which you felt anger. Reflect on these situations, being aware of who was there and what you were doing. Recall how you behaved and what you said to yourself about what was happening.

As you review these different angering situations, begin to notice the things about you that are similar across these different experiences. Notice if there is a familiar or similar story that you tell yourself about what is happening across these situations. Are there behaviors that you repeat when you get angry? Look closely and be honest with yourself.

Begin to list the things you tell yourself and the behaviors you engage in. Begin to describe this character, this sense of you, as it appears. You can use film characters or any other character if it helps. Who do you become when you're angry? What is this identity that captures you and steals your freedom? Write about the character in the space provided.

_____

_____

_____

_____

_____

Now that you have described this character, this identity, notice your emotional reaction. Write about your reaction.

_____

_____

_____

_____

_____

Now list each of the other identities you have or roles you play in your life, including the anger character just described (give the character a name and include it in the list below). Include as many as you can think of.

My identities (examples: husband, wife, partner, sister, brother, cook, golf player, dog lover and so on):

1.	5.	9.
2.	6.	10.
3.	7.	11.
4.	8.	12.

Finally, look at each of the characters you have listed. Notice how each one has its own descriptions and story to tell. Notice the ways that you behave when you're in these distinct roles. Also, notice how no single one of these identities defines you exactly, even though each identity is a description of you. Remember, the description is not the same thing as the thing described. These are smaller parts of a broader sense of you.

As we move on from this exercise, we'll continue to focus on the notion that the description and the thing described are two separate things. As you listed each of the different descriptions you have of yourself, and as you recognized that no single one of these descriptions can sum up who you are, we would add that *none* of them can sum up who you are. You might say, "Well, who am I then?" If you are not these identities more broadly and not your anger identity specifically, what's left? Who are you?

The Larger You

We've observed that human beings learn to describe and name their experiences from an early age. So, for instance, you can label an image of a past experience as *a memory*. You can label sensations on your skin with such words as *itch* or *tickle*. You can identify a thought about yourself and the world. You can label your feelings, noting if you are sad, happy, or angry. This ability to define your experiences across time and place allows you to begin to describe the "small selves" you just identified. You can label and categorize aspects of you. And, indeed, you are taught that this is what makes you, *you*.

This kind of learning helps you describe the character you developed in the exercise that stands for your anger. Painful struggles can appear when you get locked into or attached to this description of yourself. You might also find yourself behaving in ways that match that description, perhaps part of what you discovered in exercise 6.1; for example, *my angry self throws things or storms away*. Or *my angry self hides and never expresses herself*.

We all get locked into and attached to descriptions of ourselves. We all engage in behaviors that match those descriptions. Some of these attachments may not necessarily be problematic. They can even be helpful. For example, if Lisa views herself as *wise* because she knows a lot about the news and *true* because when she delivers the news she does so without expressing her own opinion, she might become a popular and trusted newscaster. However, as described, if Lisa is always in the role of a newscaster or attaches to this identity in a significant way, she will begin to experience costs. It isn't helpful to go around reporting the news all the time. Indeed, she may come across as a tiresome know-it-all. And if Lisa were asked, "Why do you report the news all the time?" she might say, "Because I am a newscaster," buying into her identity and failing to recognize the know-it-all quality it can present in other contexts. But remember, this description of Lisa and the thing being described—Lisa—are two separate things.

Not separating the thing being described and the description can cause problems for you and others attached to their identities. For instance, if you describe yourself as or hold yourself to be the angry character you developed in exercise 6.1, you may fall into the trap that Lisa does when she becomes attached to *newscaster* and experiences the costs of being considered a know-it-all. You may believe that, given this description of you, you have no other alternative but to behave the way that character behaves. You might even find yourself giving reasons and explanations supporting the behavior that comes with being angry. You likely maintain these behaviors because they make you more powerful or less vulnerable. Let's take a closer look.

Exercise 6.2: Identifying the Behaviors of Your Angry Character

In this exercise, we invite you to take a closer look at the behaviors that come with the character you created in exercise 6.1. First, write the name of this character:

"Angry you" character: _____

In the table, list the behaviors that the "angry you" character does when you are fused with this sense of you, with this identity. Also, on a scale of 1 to 3, rate how compelled you feel to do that behavior when you are "locked" into this character.

Scale

       1 = *I am in control of my behavior; I do not feel compelled to do this action.*

       2 = *I am in control sometimes, and I sometimes feel compelled to do this action.*

       3 = *I am not in control of my behavior; I feel compelled to do this action.*

Behavior that you do when you are locked into or fused with your angry character	Rating
Example: I raise my voice.	3
1.	
2.	
3.	
4.	
5.	
6.	
7.	

Reflect on the behaviors you listed and notice how tied these behaviors seem to be to the "angry you" character. It's almost as if the character and the behavior are the same things, just like the description and the described thing seem to be the same thing. But let's examine this more fully. Perhaps the identity and the behaviors are separate as well, and there is a you who knows both, yet is neither. There is a you larger than your identities, including the angry you. That same you has the power to observe thoughts, feelings, sensations, and identities without acting on a single one.

The Observer Self

If you are not who you describe yourself to be, then, as just asked, *who are you?* If you are more than these many different smaller parts of you, then who or what are you? Here, we'd like to introduce you to something we call the *observer self.* It is challenging to describe the observer self because it is beyond description.

The observer self is much larger than any of the different, smaller parts of ourselves. The observer self is the part of us that is aware of all the descriptions or identities we have about ourselves. It is the part of you that *knows* that you have distinct roles in your life or diverse identities. It is the part of you that is aware of your thoughts, feelings, senses, and behaviors. The observer self could be called awareness itself.

Contacting your aware observer self is incredibly important. It is through awareness that change is possible. If you are more than the smaller parts of you, if you're not the individual stories (and their accompanying emotions and sensations) described, then you can find freedom from them. You can be aware of your experiences without acting on them. That is, you can observe your experiences as just that: your experiences. You are the place where experiences occur, but you are not the experiences themselves. From this perspective, you can be aware of anger and not behave in costly ways. By contacting this broader sense of you, you can gain freedom from your attachments to your identities. Instead, your identities, along with your thoughts, feelings, and sensations, occur in a particular place called the observer you.

Said differently, you are not the content of your experience—you are not merely your thoughts or feelings. You are not only your sensations or descriptions. You are not the things you see with your eyes, or the images that pass through your mind. You are more than these things and more than the sum of their parts. Most important of all, you are not your anger. The observer self is the place from which you can observe all of your experiences, including but not limited to anger. It is the space in which these experiences dynamically occur. You can access this sense of you, this psychological space, by becoming aware of your ability to be aware. Let's discover this sense of you.

Exercise 6.3: Contacting the Observer Self: The Sky and the Weather

This exercise has two parts.

Part I. Begin by finding a quiet place where you can sit comfortably and close your eyes without distraction. First read the instructions below and then sit for several minutes, imagining what the instructions are inviting you to do. If you choose, and you have blue skies outside while you're doing this exercise, feel free to go out and look up at the sky as you do this exercise. You can set a timer if you like. After a few minutes, you'll open your eyes and write about your experience. (An audio version of this exercise is available at http://www.newharbinger.com/46530.)

> Imagine you are looking up at the blue sky. Notice its amazing color, its vastness, and how it stretches out in all directions. Take a minute or two to simply take in the blue sky and its eternal nature.
>
> Now imagine that you could become the sky, that you are this vast and open space. Let yourself connect to the experience of becoming the sky as much as possible.
>
> As you continue, imagine that your thoughts (descriptions), feelings, sensations, and identities (small selves) are the weather. Notice how the weather changes. The clouds come and go, the storms come and go, the lightning flashes and then stops flashing. White fluffy clouds form and dissolve; light drops of rain are blown through the sky. Sunshine streams down.
>
> Notice that as the sky you always remain, even with each of these changes. The weather changes continually, yet the sky stays. Also, notice that no matter how bad the weather gets, it cannot harm the sky. The mightiest thunderstorm, the most turbulent hurricane, the most severe winter blizzard—these things cannot hurt or harm the sky. No matter how bad the weather, the number of clouds, the fiercest winds, the sky always has room for it all—and, eventually, the weather always changes.
>
> Sometimes you can forget that you are the sky, but you are always there as the sky. The clear continuous sky is still there, stretching in all directions, boundless and pure. This is the observer you, the place where experience occurs. The sky is not the clouds, storms, or wind, and you are not your thoughts, feelings, sensations, or identities. You "hold" these, just like the sky holds the clouds, but you are not these. You are more than your experiences.

Write about your experience of contacting this part of you, awareness itself.

1. What did you notice?

   _____

   _____

   _____

2. Were you able to observe thoughts and emotions as separate from you?

   _____

   _____

   _____

3. How do you think contacting this larger sense of you, the observer, can help you with your anger experience?

   _____

   _____

   _____

Part II. Now imagine a situation that usually triggers anger for you. Imagine that you can simply be aware of it from the observer's perspective, as if that anger identity were only a smaller self, a storm, currently being held by the sky. Observe the full situation from this perspective, noticing that you are more than your anger identity, allowing this storm to come and go, to rise and fall, without any need to act on the experience, simply seeing it for what it is. Take a few minutes to let yourself notice the experience without attachment, without falling into the angry character; simply allow and be aware. When you're done, write your responses to the question.

1. What did you notice as you stayed in the observer while experiencing the storm?

   _____

   _____

   _____

2. Did you find that you were able to be less pulled to behave in costly ways? Or, said differently, were you able to be aware without falling into the anger identity? If you were, please describe. If you weren't, what do you think happened? Did you get fused and lose the experience of the observer/sky?

_____

_____

_____

We hope you could contact, if even for a moment, a broader sense of you that is aware of your experience. From this place, there is room to choose to behave differently. Since you are not your anger identity, you also do not have to be compelled to act as if you are.

Ultimately, suppose you could contact this sense of yourself more regularly. In that case, you might find that the observer self allows for the possibility of a more helpful perspective—you can defuse from troubling thoughts and feelings. You can recognize a sense of self that is constant, like the sky, and able to hold transitory phenomena: the clouds, storms, wind, and so on. This is a place from which you can observe your experience without being caught up in it. In this space, thoughts and feelings do not control actions. This facilitates conscious choice—a subject we'll turn to more fully in chapter 8, which explores committed action.

Open and Aware Living

Now that we have introduced you to a larger sense of self that is an observer of your experiences—thoughts, feelings, sensations, and so on—the question of who you are becomes less appealing. No answer is satisfactory, because whatever you say, it isn't you anyway. Instead, the better question to ask of yourself is: How do you want to be? Living openly with acceptance of your emotions and thoughts, while also being aware of these experiences, allows you to live differently. You are no longer enslaved by your thoughts and emotions. You are no longer enslaved by anger. You are free to behave in ways that are consistent with your values. You can engage in open and aware living.

It takes practice to live while being aware of your experiences, not acting on the experiences that lead to costly behavior, your anger, and/or identities derived from anger (as you recorded in exercise 6.1). To live your life mindfully aware of yourself as the sky, or yourself as the observer, will require regularly slowing down and reconnecting to this sense of you in the moment. You'll find this requires living in the present moment and being aware of your experience. Practicing awareness takes effort, but the payoff can be huge. You will own your anger instead of your anger owning you. Imagine the possibilities!

To help you practice, here's another observer-self exercise.

Exercise 6.4: Contacting the Observer Self: Whole and Stable

Find a quiet place where you can be comfortable. Read the full exercise and then follow the instructions. You can close your eyes or leave them open. (An audio version of this exercise is available at http://www.newharbinger.com/46530.)

Start by focusing your attention on your breath. Let your attention rest there, noticing the sensations that arise.

As you attend to your breathing, also notice who is noticing this breathing. There is a "you" there, observing yourself breathing. Gently open your attention to encompass the fact that your breathing has been there all along: you were breathing last week, and you were breathing a year ago. You have been breathing your whole life, and there is a you there that knows or is aware that you breathe.

Expanding your attention from your breath to your body, notice that your body senses and experiences emotion. Let yourself be aware of all of the different senses and emotions you have experienced, including those associated with anger and anger itself. Let yourself be aware of the emotions that lie under the anger. Also be aware that you have felt joy and love and happiness. You have been sensing and feeling emotion your whole life.

Expanding your attention again, allow yourself to become aware of some of the various places you have traveled to in your life. Consider the different climates that you were in or the different seasons. As you notice these places and seasons, also notice that there is a you there, a broader sense of you, that knows that you were there then and you are here now.

Shifting your attention again, focus on your memories, and think about things you have done in the past year. Stretching back in time, think of some of the things you have done in the past five years. Feel free to recall some parts of your adolescence and childhood. As you travel back in time, notice who is aware that you are remembering. Notice that there is a you there looking across time as you travel back, recalling these memories. A larger sense of you is watching them, aware of them. This observer self has been there in every situation and in every breath and is here now. This sense of you stretches across time and space. This sense of you is stable and whole. This sense of you is awareness itself.

Now write your reactions to these questions:

1. What did you notice as you engaged in the exercise? What came up in your body and mind?

    _____

    _____

    _____

2. From this place of stability and wholeness, how do you want to show up in your life?

    _____

    _____

    _____

3. From this larger sense of awareness, can you experience a sense of freedom from the harmful actions associated with anger? If you allow this possibility, what might you be able to do differently?

    _____

    _____

    _____

When you do not collapse into anger, and you can observe your experience from a place of awareness, you can notice a broader sense of self that is always there; it has always been there, a sense of self that is permanent and whole, which anger can no longer control.

Summary

The larger sense of self or awareness affords freedom. From this place, you are not your thoughts, feelings, sensations, and identities. Instead, there is a sense of you that has always been there for all your experiences, a stable and whole sense. You can choose who you want to be and the life you want to have, from your feet up, when you recognize this place. And it is your actions that finally will show the person you want to be. From this place, you can live open and aware. Behavior can change. Now, what will the behavior change be about? Instead of asking who you are, asking *how you want to be* is one way to make positive life change so that anger is no longer your master. To that end, in the next chapter we turn to values-based living.

CHAPTER 7

What Truly Matters

Sometimes everything has to be inscribed across the heavens, so you can find the one line already written inside you. Sometimes it takes a great sky to find that first, bright and indescribable wedge of freedom in your own heart.

—David Whyte

Mary is thirty-two and has cerebral cancer. She has had multiple surgeries and is undergoing chemotherapy. Mary has been in a long-standing relationship with Rick. Her family lives far away, and they have been unable to support her while receiving cancer treatment other than phone calls. Besides, Mary is used to being on her own, is self-sufficient, and insists on her independence. The challenge of cancer has tested her capacity to remain self-reliant. She has never been met with such difficulties and finds that she struggles with her new and unfamiliar condition of needing help. Mary gets quite angry about this seeming dilemma and tends to treat Rick poorly when he offers assistance. For instance, Rick offered to drive Mary to the doctor. She replied angrily, "I am not stupid or paralyzed! I can do this on my own!"

Mary is angry about what is happening to her, and she is angry for feeling vulnerable and needing help. She is afraid of dying. So Mary is pushing Rick away even though she loves him and wants him to be a part of her life. At times she worries that she will have little to offer following her treatment. She fears hurting Rick and losing her independence.

Nonetheless, when she is present, connecting to what matters to her most, she can connect meaningfully with Rick. Mary cherishes these moments and is grateful that Rick is patient with her. During these times, Mary finds a life worth living and is motivated to make a change concerning her angry behavior.

Finding Your Life Compass

Anger has a personal cost. It compromises our relationship with ourselves. And generally speaking, it compromises our relationship with others. In interpersonal relationships, anger takes on meaning, and the costs of anger, acted on in harmful ways, proliferate. Even if we are angry at those we do not know or who are not close to us, we are still relating to them in an interpersonal way. We are frustrated by their behavior, often evaluating it negatively. Anger at those we care for and love can have even higher costs.

Nevertheless, it is essential to remember that conflict and anger are universal, even in the closest relationships. Feelings of anger are inevitable. Indeed, anger in intimate relationships isn't necessarily a bad sign. As we have been exploring throughout the earlier chapters, it isn't the anger itself that is the problem, but how you relate and react to anger. For Mary, the anger has become problematic because she is letting it push her around. She is yelling and being demanding. It is causing difficulty in her most valued relationship. It is costing her something she wants—a loving relationship with Rick.

Mary can work on her relationship with anger by opening up to her vulnerabilities. As we have been working on in the previous chapters, she can learn how to wake up to her reactive style, open to her feelings of vulnerability, defuse from her thoughts, and allow her feelings and bodily sensations to rise and fall. She can learn to hold lightly her *painfully independent* identity, becoming aware of her definition of herself as self-sufficient and choosing instead to not let attachment to this idea of herself keep her from getting the help she needs. From this open and aware place, Mary has a choice—and so do you.

You, too, after practicing what you have learned from previous chapters, have a choice about how you respond to yourself, others, and the world. If anger is no longer pushing you around, seeming to lead to explosions or suppression, then what will guide you as you move forward? We are headed there now. With this chapter you will explore your life compass, finding the meaning that will guide you in changing your behavior to reflect what matters most. We'll be clarifying and defining your values. Like Mary, you have the potential to be driven by something far more profound than the passing feeling of anger. For Mary, this would mean being guided by love. When you create space for your experience and live consciously, you can freely choose your path.

Exploring Personal Meaning

Anger is part of a set of complex emotions essential for us to function in some aspects of our lives. For instance, it can help us know when there's some obstacle to meeting our needs. Anger can arise naturally out of these frustrations. This natural experience is not our enemy unless we let it rule our behavior. When we get hijacked in this way, we get pulled off course. We are no longer following the compass of our meaning. We try to control our experience by acting out or suppressing. We seem to be possessed by the emotion, and we suffer as a result. But as you have been learning here, there is an alternative.

As you continue to practice the work from earlier chapters, remembering to pause and deepen your presence in the moment, you will more readily interrupt the patterns of behavior linked to anger. You can then begin to live more consciously, occupying a larger sense of your being—a whole and stable being. From this broader perspective, wherein you are more than your anger, your values can guide your actions. The questions become: What will you choose if anger is no longer dictating how you act? What will your behavior be about instead?

Here, we invite you to explore personal purpose or meaning. What will you create through your actions that represents what you want to stand for in life?

Exercise 7.1: Contacting Your Meaningful Moments

In this exercise, we invite you to recall a few of your peak memories, those special moments in your life that you have come to cherish. You'll visit different periods in your life, and for each time point remember as fully as possible events that felt special for some reason. Perhaps you felt alive and vital, or particularly present and connected. Choose a memory that you cherish for each period, even if something painful was happening during that time. Once you have the memory, you can take your time to fully remember the event. Connect with whatever was happening at that time. You may wish to close your eyes to visualize the memory more clearly. Let yourself be immersed in the memory, recalling the sights, sounds, and emotional experiences present during that time. After each memory you are invited to write about your experience.

Time Period 1: Choose a cherished memory from childhood. After exploring the memory, write about it.

_____

_____

_____

_____

Time Period 2: Choose a cherished memory from your teenage years. After exploring the memory, write about it and your experiences. Include thoughts, sensations, and emotions:

_____

_____

_____

_____

_____

Time Period 3: Choose a cherished memory from your adult years. After exploring the memory, write about it and your experiences. Include thoughts, sensations, and emotions:

_____

_____

_____

_____

_____

Now reflect on each of these three memories and consider what made them so treasurable. Do these memories highlight some thing or things that really matter to you? See if what is happening in these memories is what makes life meaningful for you. Are there commonalities among the memories—any themes that are particularly important to you? If so, write about this here. See if your values begin to unfold as you look at the meaning beneath the memory

_____

_____

_____

The things that you wrote are the seeds of what we call values. They reflect what is valuable for you. If you're having difficulty finding the words to describe what matters to you or what is meaningful about these memories, first look ahead at the list of values words in exercise 7.2, then return to this exercise. Seeing your values emerge from these memories is part of clarifying them more fully.

This chapter presents a key question: Will your life be guided by internal experiences like anger, or will your life be guided by your values? In taking time to remember these cherished moments, you can find what matters to you most. You can see what is meaningful in your life and begin to define your values. Understanding what you care about can guide your future actions.

While our emotional experiences rise and fall, our essential values (not interests or enthusiasms or appetites, but values) are constant. Values are like a compass direction. They always point you to your true north, to what is meaningful for you in life. Emotions come along for the ride. Indeed, following your values compass direction will invite all manner of emotions—both joy and pain. Let's learn more.

Values-Based Living

Values give our lives direction, meaning, and purpose. They guide us away from emotion-driven behavior and toward spending our precious energy and moments on what truly matters to us. The importance of values-based living becomes even more clear when we consider our own finitude.

Life Is Short

The writer Stephen Vincent Benet observed, "Life is not lost by dying, it is lost minute by minute." This may seem a terrible truth, but we move closer to our own death with each passing moment. Life *is* short, and the awareness of our own death is part of what helps orient us to what is meaningful in life. If there is one fact of life, it is that we all will die. We bring this up not to be morbid or dark, but to point to something meaningful: how we'll behave in the time we have to live.

It could be argued that time is more valuable than the money or possessions we spend time obtaining. Indeed, we each want more time. Yet it continues to pass. We can never own or control time. We might wish to "buy time" or to "steal some time," but time cannot be bought or stolen. It passes with or without our consent. Given this inevitable fact, we are left with only one question about time: How will we spend it?

How we spend our time becomes an incredibly important question when considering the impact of anger on ourselves and those we care about. How we behave and what we do with our time defines our sense of meaning and purpose. Our actions signify our values. So here are some more critical questions: How will you spend your remaining time? Will you spend it creating what matters to you most?

When you relinquish the struggle to rid yourself of anger, when you turn away from acting out or suppressing anger, you're free to turn *toward* values-based living. You do not need to resolve anger and the emotions lying beneath it. You can live your values today. You can live them now.

Let's take a closer look at the qualities of values as you start this values-based journey.

Qualities of Values

One essential quality of values is that they are never-ending. They endure across time and will always be there to be lived in the time you have. It can be helpful to describe them as the directions on a compass. If you were to follow a compass and head east, you would never actually arrive at the place called east. On this round globe of ours, you can always keep going east. In somewhat the same way, you can never *achieve* your values. You can only continue to do things that stand for your values, engaging them repeatedly as you move through life.

Values are a constant source for finding a direction in life and understanding how you want to spend your time. For example, suppose you value being a good parent or friend. In that case, you are never really done being a good parent or a good friend. There are always more good parenting and more good friendship things that you can do in the different moments and contexts of your journey. Anger, whether acted on or suppressed, unfortunately can stand in the way of these qualities, seeming to shortchange the experience of values-based living—getting in the way of the direction in which you might like to head.

Understanding that values are like directions can be helpful in two ways. First, it will help you know the difference between a value and a goal. Second, you can always choose to head in a particular direction, even when things are hard or personally challenging, because values are a process.

THE DISTINCTION BETWEEN VALUES AND GOALS

Unlike a value, a goal can be achieved. If you're heading east and your goal is to stop in Lincoln, Nebraska, along the way, then you can achieve that goal. You can arrive at Lincoln, Nebraska. But east will remain in front of you if you're following that compass point. If you are working on a value of being loving, the goal might be to say "I love you" to the person you want to be loving with. If you are fused with anger—so you perhaps act out in a nonloving way or withdraw from your loved one—the goal, and an opportunity to live the value, are missed. Remember, life is always passing by—and it is short.

Here's one way to distinguish a goal from a value: you can check a goal off a list. It can become a task completed. It may take time, if it is a long-term goal, yet it can be achieved. Small or short-term goals count as well. Each can be accomplished.

Let's look at an example of a goal linked to a value. If someone holds a value of being kind, they can set a goal that represents that value. It might be something like giving a gift, or saying hello to a neighbor, or thanking the store clerk while looking at them in the eye at the checkout stand. Any of these three goals that represent the value of being kind can be reached. The gift can be given, the hello can be said, and the thank-you while looking in the eyes accomplished. Nonetheless, there will still be more kindness to do.

Imagine that you're working on one of the values you discovered in exercise 7.1. Write the one you would like to consider here:

_____

Now see if you can create a list of goals that would represent that value. Remember, they are things that can be carried out or attained. Keep in mind that these are behaviors you're engaging in to make your values come alive. Write the list here:

Goals linked to my chosen value	
1.	4.
2.	5.
3.	6.

We'll continue to explore goals, and behaviors linked to those goals, in chapter 8 when we focus on committed action. Here, we introduce you to the possibilities of living a values-based life by first clarifying some of your values and then noticing qualities of values. Values are a process. This means they are always there to be lived, no matter how long you're alive.

CHOOSING TO LIVE YOUR VALUES

Living your values is always a choice. At any point in time, you can choose to engage in values-based behavior. This becomes particularly important when you consider how anger, either acting out on it or suppressing it, can pull you away from what you want to stand for in life. As we've noted, anger can seem to steal your values from you. It can grab hold of you and seem to cause you to hit, throw, yell, or hide, acting out or suppressing in ways inconsistent with what matters to you. However, any misstep can always be followed by the choice to reengage your values again.

As you work on letting values guide your actions, it's essential to remember that you can immediately change course if you recognize that anger has you headed in the wrong direction. Simply remember what is truly important, choose to live your values, and step back onto your values-based path. As you practice being aware of your emotion, you will be better able to choose. The less you are caught by the emotion of anger, the more freedom you will have to choose your values-based path.

You should expect to make mistakes as you begin to let values guide your behaviors. Of course, you're still going to have instances of feeling anger and perhaps acting out or hiding your anger. However, if you practice being open and aware, the anger will no longer control you; *you* will be in control of your behavior (rather than running or raging). You can choose at any moment to let values guide what you do next.

Think of something that has triggered your anger. Right at the moment of the trigger, you have a choice. Hopefully, given where we are in the book, you have been tracking your anger and practicing being aware of your emotions and sensations when this happens. Now, thinking of this incident, consider the possibilities—you are aware, you choose. For instance, if the trigger to anger is about avoidance of emotional pain or hurt, you might at that moment choose to be authentic if that is a value you hold. In this instance, being authentic would mean revealing your feelings of being hurt and talking about what is painful. You would be creating your personal meaning in that moment of the choice you made to reveal rather than act out or hide.

There is another critical aspect of choosing your values. They are yours to choose. You get to decide which values you will live out. There is no right or wrong in your choice of values. There are only consequences. Your values can be the values of your parents, or not. Your values can be the values of your friends, or not. Your values can be the values of your social community, or not. Your values can simply be your values. Which values do you choose?

If you're unsure, first return to exercise 7.1 and see what values you discovered there. You can also review the list of values below and circle the ones that fit you. If you're unsure whether one of these values is truly what you would pick, you can ask yourself: *Would I still pick this value if others could never know that it was a value that I cared about?* If the answer is yes, then it is a value you hold.

Exercise 7.2: Contacting the Broader Scope of Your Values

Circle the values you hold. Choose as many as resonate with you, and use the blanks to add any we have missed.

Loving	Kindness	Generosity
Authenticity	Adventure	Honesty
Contribution	Loyalty	Trustworthiness
Justice	Autonomy	Creativity
Respect	Curiosity	Achievement
Growth	Compassion	Determination
Persistence	Harmony	

Notice how each of these values is enduring and can be chosen at any point in life. Considering how short life is, as you continue your journey it's vital to live your life according to the values you've circled here, creating what is meaningful to you.

You'll find opportunities to live your values everywhere. Sometimes we may feel as if we are not living our values during our day-to-day routines. But each moment of your life you have choices on what actions you will take, chances to align with your values over and over again.

The Places Where Values Can Be Lived

We begin this section by saying that values can be lived anywhere. However, we want to draw your attention to the main areas where values are most meaningful for most of us: family, intimate relationships, parenting, friendships and social life, education, work, recreation and fun, spirituality, community, physical health, and the environment or nature. Perhaps take a pencil and underline the top three categories that are important to you. You may be interested in all of these categories, and that's fine. Sometimes, though, when you first plan to live your values, it is simpler or easier to start with a few life areas. Most important, we suggest you look at those categories that have been suffering as a result of anger. Starting to live your values in those areas can best help you recover, more quickly healing the wounds that anger can leave. You can always expand to more categories later.

Exercise 7.3: Exploring Your Values Through Expressive Writing

In this exercise, we invite you to write about what it would mean to engage your values more fully. We offer several questions for you to consider and respond to in writing. You can work through each item in turn or mark the question or questions that strike you most and answer those.

Do this exercise when you have a stretch of private time when you will not be interrupted. Be sure to include your emotional experience in your responses, as well as any sensations that arise in your body as you reflect on the questions. Start writing as soon as you finish reading a question, letting your natural response be your guide. Don't worry about punctuation or grammar. Just write as much and for as long as you wish. Have some paper handy in case you need more than the space provided. We hope that this values exploration will land with you in a meaningful and motivational way.

1. As you consider your values and the work you have been doing with this book up to this point, does it seem possible to live them more fully, even if you feel anger? What areas of your life would you like to breathe some life into by living your values more fully, acting on values instead of anger?

    _____

    _____

    _____

    _____

    _____

2. How important is it to you to begin to live a values-based life versus an anger-driven life? What barriers linked to anger do you think you might encounter if you start this practice today? When you consider how short life is, do those barriers change?

    _____

    _____

    _____

    _____

3. How satisfied are you with how much you are currently engaged in values-based living?

_____

_____

_____

_____

_____

4. How do you want to show up in the world daily? What do you want to stand for in the unfolding moments of life?

_____

_____

_____

_____

_____

5. If you were asked to write about the footprint created by values-based living, what would you write about what that footprint looks like today for you given your struggle with anger? Is it the footprint you want?

_____

_____

_____

_____

_____

6. Given your anger, how would you be described today by the people who are closest to you? How would you like them to describe you at the end of your life, if you could pick the description?

_____

_____

_____

_____

_____

_____

7. If you could dream with no limits, what do you want to be remembered for after you die?

_____

_____

_____

_____

_____

_____

As you reflect on your answers, we want to remind you of the hope of values-based living. It is hopeful because you can choose values to be lived at any time. This means change is possible today, and that heading in the most meaningful direction to you can be an ongoing part of your life. Let your values compass guide you.

Summary

Defining and clarifying your values is part of making long-lasting and meaningful change. The values-based work found in ACT can have a powerful impact on your life, helping you heal from the problems that angry behavior has caused. We don't want you to simply make changes related to not acting out on your anger or suppressing your anger; we also want you to connect those changes to what is most meaningful for you, to your personal purpose in life. When your behavior is linked to your values, freeing yourself from being governed by emotions such as anger, then the meaning you seek in life will begin to unfold. In this place, you are no longer merely reacting. You are taking action. You're free from the trance of anger, free to do what matters most to you in life in the precious time you have to live.

In the next chapter, we turn to the behavioral commitments needed to support the process of values-based living, allowing it to begin to unfold.

CHAPTER 8

ACTing on What Matters

Start close in,
don't take the second step
or the third,
start with the first
thing
close in,
the step
you don't want to take.

—David Whyte

Gary had finally decided to seek a therapist to work on his anger. When he began therapy, he told the therapist that he felt irritated a significant portion of the time. He described it as a long-standing feeling of something boiling just beneath the surface. Upon further exploration, the therapist learned that Gary felt disrespected by his wife and child. For years he had felt the burden of not only keeping a job but also managing the household and carrying the load of cleaning and yard work. Gary described his wife and child as "kind of lazy" and addicted to television. He often found himself cleaning the house while they watched TV. His resentment grew.

A final straw brought Gary into a session. He said that he sometimes felt like running through the house and throwing things away so he didn't have to pick them up anymore. He indeed had done so on multiple occasions when he felt rage. One day his child brought home a report card with four Fs. His son was failing school. This seemed to push Gary over the edge. He smashed the two televisions, kicked his son hard on his "backside," and sent him to his room.

Later, Gary was embarrassed and ashamed of his behavior. He recognized that the family needed help and that several things needed to change. Importantly, however, he knew he never wanted to engage in that kind of behavior again. Gary made a commitment: first, to seek help, and second, to never lay a hand on his son in anger again.

Values-Based Living

Throughout previous chapters, we have been working on how holding on to or suppressing anger keeps us hooked and stuck, perhaps even sustaining or growing the anger. The desire to control the feeling of anger or use anger to hide or avoid deeper feelings is revealed as the true crux of the problem.

Earlier, we explored how excessive and misapplied control of your thoughts, feelings, and sensations—controlling others through angry behavior or suppressing anger through hiding or withdrawal—was an obstacle to a healthy relationship with yourself and others. Control itself is the problem. However, not all control is problematic. We absolutely want and invite you to be in control of your life and your behavior. It is in this kind of control that values-based living takes place. When you're in control of your behavior, the meaning you're trying to create in life can unfold. When your emotions are in control of your behavior, acting out and suppressing take control. We are inviting you to give up the latter and engage the former.

At this point, we hope you have gained some freedom from the need to control your internal experience by working on acceptance of what you experience, defusing from thoughts, and recognizing that you can connect to a larger sense of yourself that is far more than any single story you might have about yourself or your anger. From this open position, being aware of your experiences—that you are the place where your experiences happen—we turned to explore what truly matters to you in life, clarifying and defining the values you identified in chapter 7. Now it's time to create—to bring those values to life.

Committed Action

We create our life step by step. Each moment we can choose to engage in behaviors that signify our values. This sometimes takes courage and always involves commitment. In this chapter, we explore committed action, a way of helping you enact, through your behaviors, a life that honors your values.

We are going to do this through two pathways. The first path will be about exploring and tracking what it means to engage in values-based behavior. The second path will be setting small goals that support the direction in which you want to travel, as indicated by your values compass addressed in chapter 7. The ultimate goal is to grow and engage in ever-larger behavioral patterns representing the meaning you want to create in life.

Before we begin the work that concerns these two paths, let's first take a quick look at the qualities of committed action.

A Life of Richness and Meaning

When we begin to take a more detailed look at what is most important in life and determine what we want to stand for or want to be about, we embark on a great adventure. We can take these values into the world and let our actions tell the story of the same.

Values can be acted on in different ways, depending on the context or situation. You may choose to engage in a behavior in one situation that fully represents your values but that doesn't work so well in another situation. An easy example is the value of responsibility. It may be that responsibility is essential in most contexts. However, you might also imagine that responsibility at work may be different from responsibility at play. Engaging in responsible behaviors at work is often viewed as an excellent way to live a value. Even a little excessive attention to responsibility can pay off; for example, putting in a little extra time to meet a project deadline may be truly appreciated. But if you're overly responsible during play, you might find that it isn't fun anymore; for example, if you're playing a game and constantly reminding everyone of the rules, it can become annoying. Of course, it is always a balance; total abandonment of responsibility during play can also be problematic.

Let's look at a second example. Imagine you have a value of being loving and an area in which you want to live that value is with your romantic partner. One way you might show this value is by choosing to be affectionate. Here you might readily see the importance of context. It may not be appropriate to be affectionate in all situations. But there may be many contexts where it is perfectly fine. One of the qualities of committed action that deserves your attention is this: When and where do I engage in this particular values-based action?

Knowing when and where to commit to a behavior is an integral part of living your values. For instance, if you're planning to have a conversation with someone concerning your feelings, you may want to set a time with them or ask them if the time is right. You don't want to ambush them or engage in this type of conversation at an inconvenient time. This is a very individualized process. You can see that it's essential to consider your values and how you'll act on them in the many contexts you find yourself in. You may need to experiment and be willing to try new behaviors and reflect on their effectiveness. You can also get feedback from those around you after you have tried a new behavior.

Another quality of committed action to keep in mind is that no matter what behavior you choose, values-guided actions will give rise to a wide range of thoughts, feelings, and sensations. These will be unpleasant and uncomfortable as well as pleasant and comfortable. So committed action is about doing the behavior, regardless. Even if it brings up pain and discomfort. For instance, imagine that your anger has been triggered related to family. Instead of yelling—an old behavior—you are practicing present-moment awareness, and you discover that you're feeling hurt. In that moment, you want to choose values-based living over reaction. Here you can choose to engage a couple of different behaviors depending on the context. One behavior might be (while remaining present to your emotions and thoughts) to state out loud that you need time to think and that you will return to the situation shortly. Another behavior might be to nondefensively state that you're feeling hurt. Both behaviors line up with a value of being authentic or loving. Which behavior you choose might depend on how high the tensions are in the room. If they are quite high, taking time to think and returning later might be the wiser thing to do. You'll need to experiment, and it won't always be easy. Angry thoughts, sensations, and of course the emotion are bound to be there. Remember, you can choose, but it may seem challenging.

This is the tricky part: emotions, thoughts, and sensations can be loud, and as noted, they may look like they could take over. They may seem to insist that change is hard or impossible. This process is reflected in David Whyte's poem at the chapter beginning: sometimes change can only begin with the steps we don't want to take. Behavior change can be challenging, but it can also have huge payoffs.

We recognize that you may face many obstacles as you consider acting on your values instead of acting on your anger. We'll explore some of these potential obstacles shortly. But first, some further thoughts on facing the challenges. Consider the moments you have wanted to make a change in the past but did not. Consider the moments you knew you should make a change, but a thought, feeling, or sensation seemed to prevent it. As you think about what you would like to do moving forward, notice the habitual behaviors that were just too easy to inhabit. Notice whether it just seemed easier to retreat into a quiet place by suppressing your feelings.

Exercise 8.1: Barriers to Change

Write in the space provided about the things you're considering, based on the preceding text. Write freely and expressively. Notice any resistance to change and write about that as well. Write for several minutes. Have extra paper at hand in case you need more room to write. When you finish writing, answer the question that follows.

_____

_____

_____

_____

_____

_____

_____

_____

After visiting the moments where you stayed in a habitual behavior tied to anger or played it safe by trying to not show or express anger, what do you notice when you consider truly making a change? What seems different when you consider a life guided by your values?

_____

_____

_____

_____

_____

It is essential to first clarify and define your values, but only through action does your life become rich, full, and meaningful. As you begin to make changes, remember to explore, trying new behaviors and experimenting to see which behaviors match your values and when. Track the consequences of your behavior, so you can learn what is most effective, based on what you hope to create.

Exploring and Tracking a Values-Based Behavior Path

As you begin to take the first steps related to changing your anger behavior, you will want to function as a scientist. A scientist's job is to explore and investigate a phenomenon by looking closely at it and collecting data. As your own behavioral scientist, the phenomenon of study is your anger behavior and its consequences.

It is essential to remain curious. This means asking questions about how you might make behavior change, large or small, and asking what different behaviors you could try to make the changes you desire. You may want to investigate how others handle their anger; ask about their triggers, emotions, thoughts, and sensations. Which behaviors work well, and which do not?

You may be curious about and then explore a range of changes to behavior. Here are some examples to help you think about what you could do. These are examples of smaller changes. Nonetheless, they can prove to be tough to implement, especially during your early first attempts. It will be critical to remain steadfast in your commitment to keep practicing.

Possible Behavior Changes

If you talk loudly or yell while angry, try talking softly.

If you talk fast when angry, try slowing down.

If you talk slowly and deliberately with an edge to your voice when angry, try softening your voice.

If you are impulsive when angry, walk away and do something else for a while.

If you feel overwhelmed when angry, stop and do a meditation.

If you feel guilt following an anger episode, apologize—the sooner, the better.

If you furrow your brow and purse your lips while angry, soften your face.

If you feel confused while angry, ask questions and learn more about what is happening.

If you leave the room when angry and not for safety, stay and see if you can express yourself.

If you fall quiet when angry, try saying just a couple of words.

If you seethe when you're angry, talk to someone about what is going on for you. Include your thoughts, feelings, and sensations.

If you drink alcohol or take drugs to calm down, try a meditation instead.

If you throw things when angry, sit down and place your hands flat on your lap or the chair arms. Breathe.

If you drive fast while angry, take your foot off the gas pedal and get the speedometer down to the speed limit (with cruise control, if you have it). Pull off the road if you need to. Breathe.

If you fantasize about making a situation different when angry, see if you might consider nonviolent or nonangry ways to solve it.

If you isolate while angry, reach out to a friend or someone you trust.

If you swear loudly when angry, change the word to something less offensive—change "damn it" to "darn it." (We know, it might sound funny, but it truly can help.)

There are many more examples and a full variety of behaviors that you can engage in. The possible behaviors are limited only by your imagination. No matter what, make sure they are linked to your values. This is the safest way to know whether they have the potential to be workable, given the relationships you want to create with others and yourself. Notice how many of the behaviors just suggested can support a value. Even changing the tone of your voice can be about being more loving or kind. Acting as a scientist, explore different values-aligned behaviors. A deep curiosity will help; indeed, it may even make the changes fun at times. Acting as a scientist can be like art too. Cultivating graceful or artful behavior in response to anger can be part of your journey.

Exercise 8.2: Your Behaviors and Their Alternatives

In this exercise, we invite you to create a similar list to the one just presented. Write down the many behaviors that you do when you're angry and then brainstorm their potential alternatives and put them in the second column. These should be behaviors, not thoughts, feelings, or sensations. Include only things that other people can see you do or hear.

	Behaviors I do when I am angry (use the previous list of examples to help you get started)	Possible values-based alternative behaviors I am willing to try
1	Yell at so-and-so to make sure I'm heard.	Ask what I can do to change the situation.
2		
3		
4		
5		
6		
7		
8		
9		
10		

Now look through your list of behaviors again and write yet another list of possible alternatives. Remember, you can generate more than one option for each angry behavior. Be creative and practice several behaviors. You may find that you use one and it works well, or use various alternative behaviors that help you better live your values.

	Additional values-based alternative behaviors I am willing to try
1	Speak softly and check for listening.
2	
3	
4	
5	
6	
7	
8	
9	
10	

Which of these alternatives might you be willing to try today? You can practice these even when you're not angry. See what happens following the behavior change.

Don't feel limited to just these alternatives. Feel free to write as many alternative behaviors that are values-aligned as you wish. This will give you more flexibility. It will also allow you to collect data on which ones work best, by observing the consequences of the behavior change.

This exercise was a warm-up for the larger process of implementing values-based committed actions in your life. Establishing more significant patterns of behavior change will require a little more focus and effort. But even though the smaller steps may seem small in terms of the action, they are not small in terms of their importance. Small measures regularly implemented can make a powerful and long-lasting impact.

Still, these are part of a larger journey. Values-based living applies across your lifetime and in all contexts. Stretching your behavior change into your life's different domains—family, intimate relationships, parenting, friendships and social life, education, work, recreation and fun, spirituality, community, physical health, and the environment or nature—is also part of building a life that matters.

Exercise 8.3: Your Behaviors and Their Consequences

In this exercise, we have you focus on building larger patterns of behavior linked to values. We also want you to consider the consequences of the old and new behaviors as you work; for instance, what happens right after you act out or suppress anger, or what happens right after you act on a value of kindness when you're feeling angry. Take a moment and reflect on the behaviors you do when you are angry, from exercise 8.2. Consider only those behaviors for a moment, not the alternatives. As you reflect, remember the consequences of those behaviors. We return to our Possible Behavior Changes list to provide examples of consequences that we have heard from our clients:

Behavior and Its Consequences

If you talk loudly or yell while angry (behavior), others are afraid of you and pull away (consequence).

If you talk fast when angry (behavior), others misunderstand you or feel like you're not interested in their side of the story—they will pull away (consequence).

Think about the consequences of your angry behavior, whether you act out or suppress. Write about them here:

_____

_____

_____

_____

_____

The process of writing about these should ring true to other exercises in this book. The cost of anger acted on or suppressed is high. The changes in behavior that we are inviting you to try are designed to lower or eliminate those costs. You will need to experiment to see what works, then track the consequences and collect the data, to see what patterns of behavior you want to continue to grow.

Behavior and its consequences can be complicated. Sometimes we engage in values-based behavior and don't get the result we hoped for. If someone engages in angry behavior and then apologizes, and the person we injured rejects the apology, this can be hard, perhaps discouraging. Yet values-based living is always an option—it is there for you to do—even if you see that others are not living their values. This is about your meaning and purpose, your behavior. Choose accordingly.

It is also crucial to engage in behaviors that are actually doable. Sometimes people working on changes set their behavioral goals too high. You may have heard of some impossible goals like these: "I am going to lose ten pounds in one week so I can stop being so mad at myself for gaining weight," "My goal is to never yell again," "My goal is to never drink following a bout of anger." The examples are legion. We could go on and on, but we hope you see the point. Goals need to be reasonable, attainable, and linked to values. Let's take a closer look.

Setting Values-Based Goals

Imagine that your goal is to lose weight. It is linked to a value of healthy living. So you decide in the first week that you will exercise two hours a day and eat only 600 calories a day. What is likely to happen by the end of the week, if not day three or even sooner? This type of goal setting doesn't tend to work. Slow, steady progress is what we are seeking. Lasting change comes from forming new habits, and new habits take time and dedication. When you engage in committed actions, you're committing to head in a values-based direction. The goals are the little stops along the way that tell you you're doing what you care about, creating a personally chosen, meaning-based life.

SMART Goals (see Doran, 1981) will help. This system provides an easy way to define your goals, keeping them reasonable and linked to values.

SMART goals are:

S = Specific (Is the goal concrete?)

M = Meaningful (Does this goal lead me in the direction of my value?)

A = Achievable (Can this goal be accomplished?)

R = Realistic (Is the goal obtainable? Is it something I have control over?)

T = Time-limited (Can I achieve this goal within a reasonable amount of time?)

We'll give you a chance to practice setting SMART goals next as we focus on larger behavior change patterns. Try to focus on values that help you move in a values-based direction, instead of directions driven by anger.

Exercise 8.4: Exploring Your Committed Actions Through SMART Goals

Part I. In this exercise, we'll have you work to grow your values-based behavior. As you work through this exercise, consider times when anger has pulled you away from your values, then focus on reorienting back to what is important instead of letting anger rule. Taking into account the areas that you care most about and the values you have explored in the previous chapter, spend some time exploring three different ways in which you may act according to your values and track the consequences. Follow the three steps to get a feel for it, then write about what happened.

1. First, choose a category of your life that you think needs change due to problems associated with anger (such as family, intimate relationships, work, friends, and so on). Write the category you plan to work on (choose from these suggestions or another category). Start with just one; we want you to get the hang of things before you go big.

    _____

2. Next, choose the values you want to pursue in this category. List two in the space provided. Choose one that is broader and about making changes that reflect how you want your life to be (reflect on your work in chapter 7 if necessary), and list one specific to addressing anger (the two may be related, and that's okay).

    Broader valued path (for example, *Be loving*): _____

    Value specific to addressing anger (for example, *Be thoughtful of others*): _____

    _____

3. Now, based on these values, list three hoped-for behaviors that would line up with those values. These can be broader hopes for behavior change.

    Behaviors aligned with a broader valued path (for example, *Regularly tell my partner I love them*):

    _____

    _____

    _____

    Behaviors related to addressing anger (for example, *Become a better listener*):

    _____

    _____

    _____

4. Next, turn these values and behaviors into SMART goals. Complete the table following the example.

SMART Goals	*Example:* Value: Be loving Behavior: Say I love you	*Example:* Value linked to addressing anger: Being thoughtful of others Behavior: Become a good listener
S = Specific (Make the goal concrete)	I will say "I love you" on Saturday morning after our planned breakfast.	I will listen to my friend George for five straight minutes when he calls on Sunday morning and then reflect back to him what I heard.
M = Meaningful (Does this goal lead me in the direction of my value?)	Yes, saying that I love you is an excellent way to let my partner know that I am being loving.	Yes, practicing listening will help me understand others and thus be more thoughtful of them.
A = Achievable (Can this goal be accomplished?)	Yes, it is small and doable.	Yes, it is only five minutes, followed by a reflection. This is totally doable.
R = Realistic (Is the goal obtainable? Is it something I have control over?)	Yes	Yes
T = Time-limited (Can I achieve this goal within a reasonable amount of time?)	Yes, it will be done this week.	Yes, it will be accomplished by Sunday morning.

SMART Goals	Value: Behavior:	Value linked to addressing anger: Behavior:
S = Specific (Make the goal concrete)		
M = Meaningful (Does this goal lead me in the direction of my value?)		
A = Achievable (Can this goal be accomplished?)		
R = Realistic (Is the goal obtainable? Is it something I have control over?)		
T = Time-limited (Can I achieve this goal within a reasonable amount of time?)		

We hope that working through this part of the exercise will give you the hang of the SMART goals process. You can have broader ways of living your values-based life; being in touch with these is good and often healthy. However, it is even more useful to have SMART goals. They help us bring values-based action into everyday life—filling your life with values-based committed actions and creating the life you want!

Part II. After completing the SMART goals, we invite you to pursue them. Use your discipline, build your self-efficacy, and commit to reaching both SMART goals for the next week. As you engage to meet these goals, be mindful and aware. Hold your thoughts, emotions, and sensations with acceptance and defusion. Hold the story of yourself lightly from a larger perspective, and commit to take action. Track what happens and notice the consequences.

Now to write about your discoveries. Answer these questions for each of the two values you worked on.

1. What did you track or notice about how you thought, felt, and sensed while you engaged in the behavior linked to a broader value?

   _____

   _____

   _____

2. What were the consequences? Were they as you expected? Did anything surprise you? How did you feel after the consequences?

   _____

   _____

   _____

   _____

   _____

3. What did you track or notice about how you thought, felt, and sensed while you engaged in the values-based behavior linked to addressing anger?

   _____

   _____

   _____

4. What were the consequences? Were they as you expected? Did anything surprise you? How did you feel after the consequences?

_____

_____

_____

_____

_____

Now write about what you have started to create as you begin this committed action journey.

_____

_____

_____

If you were unable to take the actions, write about what got in your way.

_____

_____

_____

_____

We invite you to continue making and keeping commitments, and repeating this exercise as many times as you like.

Over our years of work with individuals, we've realized the challenges and barriers we all face in trying to make life changes. In the next section, we'll talk about the difficulties you may have encountered while working to make a change in your life. We need to look at the barriers to change and in that process, continue to invite compassion—which we'll focus on in chapter 9.

Barriers to Committed Action and How to Get Unstuck

When making positive life changes, people commonly encounter psychological barriers. This is normal. No one can stay on track all the time. The important thing is to notice when you have stepped off the path. For instance, if you feel impatient, impulsive, or triggered, and you're noticing that these experiences are pulling you away from your barriers—stop, become aware of your experience, and let your values compass guide your next action.

Common Barriers and Strategies

It's helpful to know about some of the common barriers that get people stuck. First, it's reassuring to know that you are not alone, and second, this awareness can help you anticipate the possibility and make plans to overcome them. But please, always be patient with yourself. This is not easy work.

NEGATIVELY EVALUATED THOUGHTS

As you set out to make change, you can be sure that your mind will be involved in many ways. It may help you plan and encourage you. This is great. However, it may also begin to engage in negative thinking. This too is normal. All minds have the power to dwell in negative thought, throwing up barriers to change. Your thoughts might say, *There is something wrong with me, I can't do it, I will fail, I am too anxious,* and so on.

Getting unstuck from negative thinking is often a matter of defusion. Here you can use your tools gained in chapter 5. These kinds of thoughts do not have to stand in the way of your progress. See them for what they are—thoughts. Imagine a fish swimming in water: it may not "see" the water unless it jumps above the surface. Of course, as soon as it jumps it falls back into the water. We invite you to "jump out of the water" and see the distinction between you (fish) and your mind (water). But you will need to jump again and again. Observing the mind takes practice. We fall back into mind almost as soon as we see it. Defusing from thoughts is an ongoing process.

Sometimes other sets of thoughts may seem to prevent you from moving forward. You may recall that these types of thoughts are referred to as *reason-giving*. These thoughts might say, *It's too hard, I am too busy, This is work,* and *I don't feel like it.* The mind is a reason-giving machine. As soon as we begin to think about doing something that pulls us out of our comfort zone, it cranks out all the reasons why we cant do it, shouldn't do it, or shouldn't even have to do it. The mind is clever in this way. However, if we wait until the day our mind stops reason-giving before we do the things that really matter in life, we'll never get started. So, if fusion with negative thoughts and reason-giving are a barrier to action for you, then defuse: *Aha! Here it is again. The "I can't do it" story. Thanks, mind! But I have my life to live.* Notice the ongoing flow of thinking and take the first step.

AVOIDANCE OF DISCOMFORT

Change usually elicits uncomfortable feelings, especially anxiety. Moving forward in meaningful ways will mean accepting this discomfort. Remember, you may still have the feeling of anger—but the anger is not in charge of what you do with your feet. It is not in charge of your values-based actions. Use your acceptance skills from chapter 3.

Open up to the internal bodily experiences; let them flow through you, not become you. The feeling of anger will rise and fall. You might remember to try being mindfully aware of your bodily experience. Simply allow the feelings that arise, including the ones that anger may be covering over. You can walk forward with feelings of anger. They are natural, but again, they simply aren't in charge of what you do. Also, if there are other feelings that the anger is covering over, open up to them and, if appropriate, share them, not just the anger. Change is about walking with discomfort, including but not limited to anger. Indeed, discomfort precedes growth.

LOSS OF MOTIVATION

Loss of motivation can look like a difficult barrier to overcome. It seems different, but often it is yet another reason-giving tactic that the mind can focus on. You might hear your mind say, *I have no motivation. I just can't catch my anger. Why bother?* And, indeed, you may have low-energy feelings tied to that thought. You have tried to change your angry behavior in the past; now you may feel discouraged. However, this is no different from what we have been recommending. You can use both defusion and acceptance to guide you back to the path of values-based living. Don't succumb to any thoughts of losing your motivation. Besides, motivation tends to *follow* action, not precede it.

It's also essential to stay in touch with your values. Remind yourself of your values and your intention to create your meaning by following them. You can reengage with your values at any point. If they seem murky when you're unmotivated, you may want to continue to clarify them. Return to chapter 7, and remind yourself, reevaluate, and deepen the description of your values. Remember, your committed action goals are derived directly from your values.

ENLIST SUPPORT

Sometimes when we are making a change we can feel all alone. Especially when we are working on something personal and vital. We may be embarrassed to ask for support. However, getting help can be one of your best strategies for success.

Social support is often highly motivating. Imagine enlisting a partner, friend, relative, coworker, or neighbor with whom you can share your change aspirations and your achievements. Chances are their listening and encouragement will help make the process run more smoothly. Be sure to enlist someone who will support you. Tell them your intentions and plans. Share your SMART goals. Speak to them about your values, and check in with them regularly about your progress. Renew your commitments, share this with them, and ask for their encouragement. Be sure to share your successes with them as well as the bumps in the road.

USE REMINDERS

Another barrier to success in making change is forgetfulness. It's easy for us to forget to do what we had planned to do. We all have busy schedules and hectic lives. You have probably had the experience of intending to do something, but then a whole week passes without your remembering to do it. It happens to the best of us.

One easy solution is to create reminders. Place alerts on your phone or computer, mark out a special time in your calendar, write it in your journal (if you check it often), ask someone to remind you, or place a sticky note on the refrigerator or rearview mirror. If you have a tool that helps you remember, use that tool. These are all excellent ways to help you remember to work on your SMART goal.

EXCESSIVE GOALS

Another barrier to success in changing behavior is working on too many goals at one time. Make sure your goals don't exceed your resources—whether those be skills, time, money, or physical health—or you will end up giving up or failing. You can always start small, even if your resources are low. Remember, your SMART goals can be as small as changing your tone of voice when feeling angry.

ACCEPT BEING STUCK SOMETIMES

If you feel stuck, you can simply notice this experience. It is the same as noticing the anger or the feelings underneath the anger. This approach is far more effective than beating yourself up for getting stuck! Beating yourself up for getting stuck can actually make things worse.

In fact, we hope that encountering these barriers will be useful. You can turn these difficult experiences into opportunities to develop self-acceptance and self-compassion. For instance, if you're stuck, you might ask yourself: *Will I, as a choice, accept myself as a human being even though I am temporarily stuck? Will I, as a choice, be kind and caring toward myself instead of beating myself up?*

Being stuck, along with the practices we hope you have been implementing since picking up this book, gives you additional opportunities to *cultivate willingness.* As you practice these new skills, especially for changing behavioral patterns linked to anger, you are bound to confront difficulty and discomfort. The pursuit of goals that pull you out of your comfort zone can generate significant anxiety. In these moments, it's essential to cultivate your willingness to persevere.

Making room for discomfort may mean asking yourself: *Am I willing to feel some discomfort, to do what matters to me?* or *Am I willing to make room for sweaty hands, and a knot in my stomach, and a tightness in my chest, and a voice in my head that tells me negative things, if that's what I need to do to make room to do the things that really matter to me?*

If you are unwilling to make room for this inevitable discomfort, you may need to (1) work on acceptance skills; (2) enhance the link of your behavior to your values; or (3) set a more manageable goal, provoking less discomfort. Remember, you are building, and building is a process.

Keeping Commitments

Every moment is an opportunity to get going. It is time to begin your lifelong practice of making and keeping commitments linked to your values and changing your behavior so that anger no longer controls you. Keeping these commitments requires persistence. And getting started with one small step is all it takes.

Exercise 8.5: Make a Commitment and Take the Step

With this exercise, you'll build on the exercises already completed. Commit to a day and time to begin. Then, no matter how you feel at that time, pursue more SMART goals, ones related to the larger values you want to implement and ones related directly to the behavior change you want to make concerning anger. Use the format already provided. This is all about action and doing something different with your life. Indeed, unless you take action, nothing will change. Anticipate your barriers and be prepared. Get support if you need it.. And *go!*

Date: _____

Time: _____

SMART goal (larger values in life): _____

    S = Specific (Is the goal concrete?): _____

    M = Meaningful (Is this goal linked to a value? What is the value?): _____

    _____

    A = Achievable (Can this goal be accomplished?): _____

    R = Realistic (Is the goal obtainable? Is it something I have control over?): _____

    T = Time-limited (Can I achieve this goal within a reasonable amount of time?): _____

Date: _____

Time: _____

SMART goal (larger values in life): _____

    S = Specific (Is the goal concrete?): _____

    M = Meaningful (Is this goal linked to a value? What is the value?): _____

    _____

    A = Achievable (Can this goal be accomplished?): _____

    R = Realistic (Is the goal obtainable? Is it something I have control over?): _____

    T = Time-limited (Can I achieve this goal within a reasonable amount of time?): _____

Copy your new plan and SMART your way into values-based living. Make a commitment to continue these SMART goals linked to values in an ongoing way.

Summary

Now that you have your values-based life direction and have been exploring behavior change to get yourself started with your committed actions, we hope you are encouraged to make life better, especially as it relates to problematic anger behavior. You have worked diligently to digest this material and engage the exercises, and we hope you're proud of what you have done to date. As we have worked with people over the years, it has been our pleasure to see change, taking pride in those who follow through on their commitments. They are living life from the feet up, and this is our hope for you.

It is worth repeating: change is not always easy. Sometimes different kinds of practices need to be engaged and cultivated, and we now turn to one of those: compassion. Cultivating this practice is one of the most important ways to help you live beyond anger.

Remind yourself that each moment is an opportunity to honor what you value, and that the life you want to create is done step by step.

CHAPTER 9

Compassion and Anger

Anger is often just suffering that has not been met with compassion.

—Dalai Lama

Adrian, forty-five, has been dealing with anger problems since he was a young boy. He described himself as a "firecracker waiting to explode" even as a child, always feeling misunderstood and challenged by unfairness in life. The cost of his angry explosions grew over time, and several years ago he recognized the need to get help. Adrian worked on acceptance, defusion, present moment, and values. Over time he found that he was more able to express his emotions, not getting trapped in the content of his mind, living more fully in the here and now, and following his values to connect with others in more open and thoughtful ways. He found that he was doing well in several areas. There were no more verbal explosions at his neighbors for being noisy, his feelings of road rage were much less frequent, and his relationships had steadily improved.

Adrian was working on being more flexible by responding from a values-based position instead of being right. He had been particularly surprised by how his skillful management of situations often changed them in his favor. He was more assertive in his communication and didn't feel as triggered by issues of unfairness.

Despite this great work, Adrian still became concerned and criticized himself when he felt any anger. Feelings of anger reminded him of how he used to act. Adrian could get hooked again, becoming angry at himself instead of at others.

Throughout this book, we have been exploring different ways to have a wiser relationship with your emotions, especially anger. We hope that by now you're feeling more fluent in accepting your emotions and defusing from your mind while working on values-based living. Nonetheless, we understand how difficult it can be to make a change. Even after we take big steps to improve our relationship with ourselves and others, we can still find ourselves criticizing our behavior. You may still find yourself in Adrian's situation, lacking compassion and turning away from yourself just when turning toward yourself is needed most. Remember, thoughts do not disappear. We simply change our relationship to them. Feelings will still rise and fall. Noticing them is part of the work.

From Criticism to Compassion: Another Change That Makes a Difference

Notice that despite the changes you have made, you can still get triggered to anger. This is normal. What really matters is how you behave when it happens. It's not surprising that you still land in angry places and then criticize yourself for it. Criticism is part of a rigged game that captures all of us. Evolution, learning histories—whatever the case, we are all susceptible to a negativity bias. This is a survival-driven habit that leads us to scan for what's wrong in the world and to fixate on it. The problem is, even our inner experiences can appear to be a "lion." We are threatened by our thoughts and emotions. Let's take a closer look.

The Self-Criticism Trap

In contemporary society, a pervasive thought target that we all tend to fixate on is our own sense of unworthiness. We habitually dwell on how we're falling short—in our relationships, work, appearance, mood, and behaviors. Criticizing ourselves for not being better, faster, kinder, and so on. Given this, it's natural that feeling or acting on anger can be one more place in which we feel we are falling short. If you're working to change your relationship with your anger, and from time to time it doesn't work, or you find that even though things are working better, you are still highly self-evaluative, you may be caught in a self-criticism trap. However, the mind does what it does. It compares you to other people—*Why don't others get angry like I do?* It compares you to yourself—*Why can't I just do this all the time, like I did the other day? What is wrong with me?* Check to see if your mind has a negative, if not hostile, relationship with you when you feel unworthy or when you feel as if you are failing.

While this kind of self-aversion can be a primary (automatic, built-in) reflex, we can still get hooked, failing to recognize its automatic nature. We almost instantly go to work, criticizing ourselves in harsh and long-lasting ways. By the way, this same automatic mechanism can focus itself on the faults of others as well. We can tune in to and criticize others when we think they are doing something wrong or bad. We can insist, either out loud or in our heads, that others do things differently—that is, do things correctly according to *us*. In criticizing others, we can go down the same road of negativity and hostility that we inflict on ourselves.

Whether we are focusing inwardly or outwardly, we are creating an enemy. We imprison ourselves in criticism and start living in threat mode. There we lose access to feelings of connection, empathy, well-being, and love. We lose access to compassion, or we discover that either we didn't have it in the first place, or it is very rusty and in need of our strongest can of lubricating oil.

Compassion is a powerful antidote to self-criticism and criticism of others. It is a potent way to make a significant shift in your relationship to yourself and others, inviting a kinder, more open attitude in place of harshness and judgment.

If, for any reason, you find yourself balking at this idea of kind, open compassion, hang in there. You might find that it is one of the more effective ways to make a difference in your life and in the healing and recovery you seek concerning a history of anger.

Where to Even Begin

It may be useful at this point to look back at what we have been exploring. Remember to ask yourself, *What is behind my outburst or suppression of anger?* There could be feelings not only of hurt and vulnerability, but also of loneliness. Ask yourself if being angry isn't also quite lonely. Ask if it isn't isolating. You don't have to look too far to see these types of experiences beneath anger. These feelings can accompany the sense of being by yourself, of others not understanding or knowing your struggle or appreciating your deeper feelings. You may find an experience of not feeling loved or cared about. Suffering from criticism about your worth and failures can lead to even greater anger and pain.

The cycle of criticism and suffering begins to perpetuate itself. This can be true for your criticisms both about yourself and about others. For instance, when we see others behaving angrily or responding in inflexible ways, notice how we tend to pull away from them or leave them alone. We don't want to be around them. We do to others the very thing they do to us when we are angry. We avoid, dismiss, step away. We get away from others, just as they might get away from us. There is quite a bit of aloneness in this whole process. You are hurting. Others are hurting. Where do we even begin to do something different? Where do we begin to interrupt this cycle?

We might begin by offering compassion, the subject of this chapter. We've already been talking about it, but it's worth defining. Compassion is the concern for and desire to alleviate another's suffering (or our own—in which case it is *self-compassion*). It is about recognizing pain and offering a gentle presence and desire to relieve the pain. It is about taking a kind and loving stance toward yourself and others. A compassionate stance can make all the difference. It can help you heal from feelings of anger, sadness, shame, and loneliness in times of anger. You might ask, *How can I care and love myself when I am angry and hurting?* or *How can I care and offer love for others when I am criticizing them?* You might say we ask the impossible.

We know this may sound surprising or odd—whatever your mind may give you. Your mind might be shouting against this invitation. But hold on. Again, compassion is a powerful thing. If you begin to practice compassion for yourself and others, you may find that it awakens your full potential for natural presence and caring. You might find that it heals. Indeed, the benefits of compassion have been well studied, and it's now known that it improves people's lives, health, and well-being (a topic we'll explore more shortly).

When you begin practicing compassion, the first thing to do is recognize that vulnerability and feelings of sadness, shame, and anger are not weaknesses, nor something to be criticized. We each experience our own level of fear and pain. And when we get hooked by anger, it seems to drive us to behave in ways that we didn't intend. We blame others or ourselves. We act out or suppress. We can forget to stop and look at what is driving the anger. We forget to look at what is going on underneath. Is it insecurity, fear? Is it sadness? Is it being caught up in thoughts of who is right and who is wrong? The anger serves its purpose in that it hides our feelings of vulnerability. However, whatever the hiding looks like, we can feel shame and begin to criticize ourselves for the whole experience of anger and pain. The cycle is now in motion.

But when you understand that you are hurting in some way, that you want something—perhaps acceptance or love—you may naturally open up to a kinder place, stepping out of blame and into self-compassion.

Furthermore, when criticizing others just after (and even during) an angry incident, if you begin to acknowledge your fears here as well, compassion can win the day. Once you are more present and balanced, you can look at what might be behind their behavior with eyes of wisdom and knowing. Ask yourself, *How might this person be caught in their own sense of insecurity, inadequacy, confusion?* If you can begin to see how this person might be suffering, you might reconnect with a natural sense of tenderness and care. This is the road of compassion.

Compassion provides an alternative to focusing on shame and criticism. It teaches us ways to be with ourselves and others when we suffer, and as the Dalai Lama says: "Anger is often just suffering that has not been met with compassion."

Building Compassion

Compassion entails allowing ourselves to be moved by suffering—both our own and the suffering of other people. Compassion is also about committing to a desire to help, to take away the suffering of the self or other. This is not always easy to do. Sometimes we feel we don't deserve compassion. Sometimes we don't remember to be more compassionate. Compassion takes courage—the courage to face the things that make us uncomfortable and sometimes the courage to face the things that scare us most about ourselves.

Compassion in Two Parts

Compassion involves two major parts: (1) openness, sensitivity, and caring for ourselves and others' suffering and pain, and (2) the motivation to reduce suffering. It offers a way of being gentler and kinder to ourselves or others in the presence of the suffering and pain of anger or blame.

Compassion is a different way of dealing with suffering and emotional pain than we may be used to. Indeed, in our culture we often receive messages that are the opposite of compassion. If we are hurting or in pain, the cultural message tells us there is something wrong with us. If we are having a difficult time, we tend to think it is our (or someone else's) fault. We feel we must deal with it by crushing the emotional experience associated with being wrong or at fault. If others are experiencing emotions like fear or sadness, it typically is taken as an indication that they are weak, perhaps undeserving of sympathy. In the absence of compassion, we view vulnerability, loneliness, pain, sadness, or anger as problems to be solved instead of experiences to be met with kindness and caring.

When we are facing the difficulties of living with feelings of anger and the fallout of habitually behaving in ways consistent with anger, a compassionate approach doesn't seem possible. But it is always possible—it just looks quite different from what you're used to. With a compassionate stance toward yourself and others, you recognize that life is filled with difficulties. We all will feel pain, fear, sadness, anger, loss, grief, and other emotional challenges. Compassion recognizes that these are not signs of weakness, but normal human experiences. As we have already seen in previous chapters, avoiding, denying, or otherwise refusing to acknowledge and work with these difficulties produces more suffering and problems.

So developing a compassionate relationship with ourselves and others can help us create a different relationship with our own internal experiences. It can help us deal more kindly with our unpleasant feelings of anger, sadness, and so on. It can help us heal. Compassion can lead to the creation of a quite different and healthier relationship with yourself, turning to kindness instead of harshness, turning to gentleness instead of harsh criticism, turning to love instead of hate.

As with the other processes we've focused on in this book, compassion needs to be trained and developed. It needs to be cultivated. We cannot simply say that we want to be more compassionate and then engage in this kind of process. It takes work, practice, and patience. However, as with all forms of practice, there is a payoff. You can *learn* to be kinder to yourself and others. Let's start the process of compassion training and see what the effect is for you.

Exercise 9.1: Compassionate Recognition of Anger as Suffering

Part I. Compassion can free us from suffering. The purpose of this exercise is to deepen your understanding that anger is a normal emotional response but that your reaction to it creates suffering. We also invite you to see what happens if you respond to suffering with compassion. Take a quiet moment and consider what it is like when you're caught up in anger. Think of a time when the fallout of anger was quite problematic, and how you felt in that moment. Read the following questions as they relate to your struggle with anger, letting your responses bloom from the memory of that time. You won't be writing answers to each question individually, but letting your responses gather. Finally, write about your response to the experience.

1. Are you truly happy with the outcome of your anger?

2. Are you comfortable with what unfolded?

3. Did you feel safe? Did others feel safe?

4. Did you feel connected with others?

5. Did your thoughts and behaviors reflect the sort of person you want to be?

6. Were the outcomes of your anger what you hoped for?

Write here your reaction to these questions. Notice whether you start to feel any shame or self-criticism arising. Notice that anger and its fallout is suffering itself.

_____

_____

_____

_____

_____

_____

Using the same moment of anger or anger situation, consider the following questions:

1. What might it take to be happy in this moment if I do not get what I want?

2. How could I feel comfortable in this moment of anger if the anger is not going away?

3. How could I feel safe in this moment of anger and pain?

4. How could I feel connected to others in this moment?

5.   How can I reflect on who I want to be in this moment?

6.   What do I hope for?

Now write your answers. We recognize that this might be more difficult than answering the first set of questions. Challenge yourself: what might help you in this situation?

_____

_____

_____

_____

_____

_____

Now look at what you've written. Did you think that criticism and blame would be helpful? We are going to take a guess that you didn't. You know that in a moment where comfort, safety, and connection are needed, criticism and self-blame are not the answer. This is a moment when something else is needed. What would happen if you could offer caring and love for yourself in this moment of anger? Imagine, if only for a moment, how that might change things.

Part II. Now consider others who are also creating suffering in the way they relate to anger. Consider that this unpleasant kind of experience is a type of suffering that affects not only you but also those you interact with. Imagine having the motivation for them to be free of their suffering. Feel this motivation and imagine how it would be to act on it. Write about your experience:

_____

_____

_____

_____

_____

_____

Just as they did for Adrian, the challenges of self-criticism and blame can still haunt you if you get angry, especially if you have been working to change your relationship to anger while becoming more vulnerable. The point is not to criticize or blame. Be aware of the suffering that comes from a lack of caring toward oneself and others. Notice that harsh words toward yourself and others don't decrease the suffering. In this circumstance, they only increase it. Your work to do here is to meet criticism and blame with compassion.

Questions about the possibility of compassion arise. Can you hold yourself with caring and kindness? Can you hold others lovingly? Let's explore how to begin to build compassion in the next exercise.

Exercise 9.2: Beginning to Cultivate Compassion

Part I. In this exercise, you'll sit in a quiet place and explore a series of images. (An audio version of this exercise is available at http://www.newharbinger.com/46530.) As you consider each one, take time to let your imagination help you fully develop the image. Moving too quickly through the exercise will undermine the cultivation process. Take two to three minutes for each numbered item, closing your eyes and letting yourself explore with your imagination. If you experience any difficulty creating the image, call to mind someone else who might represent the quality you're trying to create. It can be a real person or someone from a movie or television show. Use them as a role model.

1.   Imagine yourself as a calm and wise being. What do you picture?

   _____

   _____

   _____

2.   Imagine yourself being aware of all emotions, fully seeing what you and others feel. What do you notice?

   _____

   _____

   _____

3. Imagine yourself as confident, having the ability to tolerate difficulties. What do you see?

_____

_____

_____

4. Imagine yourself being warm and kind to yourself and others. What do you notice?

_____

_____

_____

5. Imagine yourself being noncondemning, wanting to help relieve the suffering of others. What shows up for you here?

_____

_____

_____

Now write for a moment about what you experienced as you imagined yourself as each of these different types of beings.

_____

_____

_____

Part II. For this part of the exercise, we invite you to again close your eyes, continuing to build this sense of being someone who can offer compassion. Read the following instructions, then close your eyes and let yourself engage in the exercise.

1. Allow five minutes. With your eyes closed and holding a compassionate facial expression—perhaps a half-smile of kindness—imagine yourself expanding, as if you are becoming more powerful, mature, and wise, able to tolerate pain and offer kindness.

2.   Pay attention to the sensations in your body as you develop this part of yourself. Spend a moment just feeling these sensations in your body.

When you have finished, write about the experience. Include the body sensations you noticed.

_____

_____

_____

Now let yourself consider all the qualities that you would ideally have as a compassionate person. These are the qualities you're trying to build in this exercise. Remember, this may not be easy as you first begin. Cultivating compassion can take time and may feel awkward at first. Indeed, it may even sound odd or seem uncomfortable. We are not used to being kind to ourselves in this way. But kindness and caring—compassion—are the great antidote to criticism and blame. Compassion is also quite different from anger, so the work of being kind and caring may present a welcome challenge. It is a challenge worth taking. Having compassion for yourself and others is an ideal healing process. It is the cure for suffering.

As with all of your efforts here working to free your life from being ruled by anger, cultivating compassion will take practice. Do practice often, so you can become familiar with this type of healing. The more you practice, the more easily you can access your own natural capacity for compassion, and the more readily you can offer it when you're struggling.

Now that you have begun to imagine a sense of self that can feel compassion, continue cultivating this experience. Don't worry if you have not developed this sense of you from just one session of exercise 9.2. You can go back and do it as often as you'd like. Each time try to let yourself experience each of the suggested visualizations. With a little persistence, this sense of you will begin to develop. Let's continue to grow your sense of compassion through another exercise.

Exercise 9.3: Growing Your Compassion

Find a quiet place to reflect, and give yourself about ten minutes to complete the full exercise. First read through the instructions (more than once, if necessary), then follow them. (An audio version of this exercise is available at http://www.newharbinger.com/46530.)

1.   Bring to mind a situation in which you recently struggled with anger or the fallout from anger (self-criticism or self-blame). Write the situation you have chosen here:

_____

_____

2. Be sure you've already read this guided visualization, then close your eyes and imagine the situation as follows:

Let yourself get in touch with the feeling you experienced during the event, as much as possible. Once you have a good sense of the feeling, imagine that a much younger version of you was feeling the same way. Then imagine that you could see this younger version of yourself as if you were standing outside of this version, looking back at yourself. Notice the feeling they are having in this moment. Notice how much they are struggling, how much they are suffering. Take your time and let yourself really take in what you see—a younger version of you feeling this badly, having this much anger, or this much criticism and self-blame. Notice if you have any desire to reach out and help. Notice what this younger version of you needs. And now, bring the compassionate part of you that you developed with exercise 9.2 into the scene. Become that sense of you that is calm, wise, confident, and courageous. Become that sense of you that is compassionate. From this perspective, how would you understand what is happening here with this younger sense of you? What does this younger sense of you need? If you could whisper into the ear of this younger you, feeling as they do, what support or encouragement might you offer? Is there some kindness and caring you might extend to this younger self? See if you can relate to this younger self as you would relate to someone you dearly care about and want to help. See if it's possible to experience the powerful feelings and thoughts the younger self is having not as something wrong but rather as something quite human in the face of difficulty. See if you can continue to extend this sense of caring and kindness for a few minutes.

3. Open your eyes and write about your experience:

_____

_____

_____

_____

_____

When Adrian did these two exercises, he felt teary-eyed and vulnerable. He realized that for a long time he had been having a hostile relationship with himself following times of anger. He had been condemning himself for the way he used to behave. After completing the exercises, he could see the hurt he created with this kind of relationship with himself. Even though he thought he deserved the criticism, Adrian learned that criticism only made it worse. Adrian also noticed that he felt uncomfortable at the beginning of starting to cultivate compassion, even "silly" at times. With practice and persistence, however, he learned that compassion was transformative. He appreciated the opportunity to be kinder and more caring toward himself, noticing that the suffering decreased. This made it easier to turn his attention toward his values and engage in meaningful behaviors instead of sulking in anger or self-criticism.

We hope that with practice you will be able to cultivate compassion and ease your own suffering, freeing yourself to live your values as well. The next time you notice yourself filled with anger or other feelings resulting from anger, instead of simply trying to muscle through it with criticism and blame—trying to whip yourself into shape—take a moment and compassionately acknowledge what is happening. Be aware of your internal experience. Notice, *Wow, I'm really angry right now. I'm really struggling. This is really hard. I'm suffering.* Then offer compassion, connecting kindly and caringly with that suffering part of yourself.

Growing Compassion

Remember, to cultivate means to acquire or develop—to grow. There are many different ways that you can develop a compassionate practice. Continue to practice what we have suggested here, and grow your practice by listening to and engaging in additional compassion exercises—you can find them on the internet or in app stores.

Actively Expressing Compassion for Yourself

Once you have begun to allow compassion to arise, the next step is to actively express it. This is what brings compassion fully to life. Continue to offer compassion to yourself, especially when you feel vulnerable. What does the part of you that feels anger, pain, shame, and so on actually need? Is it forgiveness? Acceptance? Companionship? Safety? Love? Whatever it is, from your most calm and wise place, offer kindness and caring. Either mentally or with a whisper, you might say your name and send a message, telling yourself that you are holding the suffering with love, that you're not leaving. You might place a hand gently on your heart or cheek or even give yourself a light hug as a way of conveying, from a compassionate place, *I'm here with you. I care.*

Actively Expressing Compassion for Others

As we have been noting, not only do we too often treat ourselves harshly following acts of anger, but we can also treat others with harsh judgment, especially if we are blaming them for sparking the anger in the first place. The harsh judgment of others might also be part of the whole anger process. When others don't act as we wish, or fail us in some way, we might judge them. In these moments, we forget that they are also human beings with their own measure of suffering. We forget that they struggle too. Every person experiences vulnerability and wishes to be accepted and loved. Growing your compassion for others is part of building a more compassionate stance toward yourself.

Building compassion toward others doesn't mean that it is okay for others to hurt you or that you should not act to stop them. But those actions are different when they come from a place of harsh judgment than when they come from a place of compassion. One of the best ways to test this difference is to give it a try. But first, let's look closer at what might be needed.

When we offer compassion to others, empathy is essential. Empathy involves working to understand other people's perspectives, particularly their emotional experiences and motivations. You might ask yourself the following questions when you find that you're judging another or when someone has hurt you: *Why might they be behaving in this way? What might they be feeling? What might they be thinking? Is there a way in which this behavior makes sense if I take a different perspective?* Your answers might help you call on compassion to guide your response.

Remember, just as life can be difficult for us, filled with tough experiences and hard choices, so it is for everyone else. When we find ourselves struggling at times, we may simply want to be free from suffering. Psychologist and author Marshall Rosenberg captured this sentiment when he observed that every criticism, judgment, diagnosis, and expression of anger was actually expressing an unmet need. Compassion and empathy are about acknowledging what is happening from our own perspective—but also taking the perspective of others. When we begin to build a more nurturing and kinder communication between ourselves and others, we also build understanding—a perfect counter to anger.

Exercise 9.4. Compassion for Others: Loving-Kindness Meditation

Compassion and loving-kindness are like two sides of the same coin. Loving-kindness is the sincere wish that oneself and others experience peace and happiness, and the motivation to help all of us have these things. This exercise can be done in a way designed to cultivate loving-kindness toward oneself, another person or other people, or all beings. (An audio version of this exercise is available at http://www.newharbinger .com/46530.)

In this traditional loving-kindness exercise—designed to cultivate a state of kindness and warmth toward all beings—you will be led through a series of visualizations and repeated phrases. For each of the following people, you will be asked to visualize them and then repeat a set of phrases:

- A beloved other (someone you naturally and easily experience kindness and warmth toward). This will help you connect with feelings of kindness and warmth.

- Someone you feel neutral toward.

- Someone for whom you feel irritation, frustration, or anger.

- Yourself.

- All beings.

Begin the exercise by closing your eyes and bringing up images of the listed people (their face or whole body), one by one. Once you're holding the person in your mind's eye, repeat to yourself the phrases of loving-kindness that follow while trying to generate an emotional experience of kindness and warmth toward the person(s) being visualized:

- May you [or I] be happy.

- May you [or I] be free from suffering.

- May you [or I] love and feel loved.

As you repeat the phrases, work to generate goodwill by extending a sense of each and well wishes. Let a kind smile soften your face.

To complete the exercise, allow yourself to experience the satisfaction of having extended kindness and warmth. Recall that you and all other beings simply want to be happy and feel a sense of peace.

Just as you will need to cultivate compassion for yourself, you will need to cultivate it for others. It is a powerful healing tool. Offering compassion and recognizing suffering ease tension and clarify what we hope for: loving understanding.

Summary

Making the change from anger and criticism to compassion toward ourselves and others is a journey. The journey begins by recognizing our own measure of suffering and desire to lessen the suffering. This can be done. Cultivating compassion through steady and gentle practice, returning to it again and again, will ease suffering and heal old wounds and fresh pain. Be patient. Cultivating compassion takes time, and we often have to overcome the initial bumps associated with trying something new or unfamiliar. But if you hang in there, the payoff is worth the effort.

Aside from lack of compassion, another reason we struggle when suffering from anger and its fallout is an inability to forgive. Forgiveness is another powerful tool for recovering from anger. Given that anger often involves harming ourselves and others, forgiveness can lead to healing of that harm. Join us in chapter 10 as we explore forgiveness and its possibilities.

Forgiveness and Anger

Forgiveness is the key to action and freedom.

—Hannah Arendt

The way Anthony related the incident, he had simply "snapped." He and his youngest son, Matthew, now twelve, had been round and round about getting good grades. These talks and sometimes arguments had covered "all the possible reasons" for why good grades should be attained. At the end of the school year, Anthony had received a phone call from Matthew's teacher, noting that his son would need to attend summer school again. Matthew had received five Fs and a D on his report card. When Matthew got home, Anthony had laid into him about what had happened. Anthony yelled for nearly fifteen minutes and then told Matthew to go to his room. As Matthew began to march up the stairs, he made a sarcastic comment, and Anthony reacted by kicking him hard, "booting" Matthew in the behind.

Anthony had let his anger get the best of him. His son began to cry and ran to his room. Later, Anthony apologized for what had happened, telling his son that he wished he had not kicked him. Even though Matthew said that he forgave his father, Anthony could not seem to forgive himself. Anthony felt foolish and ashamed. He blamed himself for being a bad father.

Years later, when Anthony finally entered therapy, he revealed several of these types of incidents with his son. He had asked Matthew's forgiveness several times. Yet he could not forgive himself. He couldn't understand his own behavior and motivations. Anthony held simmering anger at himself for reacting so impulsively and causing his son pain. Among the other issues related to the anger he was working on in therapy, these incidents became a focal point. Anthony needed to forgive himself.

By this point in the book, we hope you have been working steadily on being open to your emotions, aware of your experiences, and actively engaged in your values. As with the last chapter, we want to acknowledge the places where those struggling with anger can still remain stuck. Just as self-criticism can continue and a need for self-compassion arises, those who have engaged in aggressive or problematic behaviors linked to anger may need to also do some forgiveness work. A companion to compassion, forgiveness is an important part of healing from the wounds of destructive behavior. In this chapter, we explore forgiveness of ourself and others.

Starting the Process of Forgiveness

As have many of us, Anthony reacted to a situation with an outburst that he regretted. Acting impulsively can lead to unfavorable consequences and feelings of guilt or shame. We can be haunted by these actions, with persistent memories of the regretted behavior and memories of how others felt and reacted. Too many of these impulsive, aggressive actions can cause permanent damage to relationships. It can also lead to a highly self-critical relationship with oneself as a form of punishment. Self-talk regarding these actions can include everything from simply calling oneself bad names to actively engaging in talk that revolves around self-hatred. If, when reflecting on your own angry behavior, you have ever found yourself thinking things like *What is wrong with me?* or *I am a horrible person* or *It's too late for me, why bother?* then you might be in a self-criticism trap. This is a difficult trap to escape, because self-criticism doesn't often lead to positive behavior change.

Other forms of self-punishment can also participate in this post-anger response. These might include withdrawal and isolation, repeated attempts to repair, and even acting like it didn't happen (though you may quietly recognize that it did). Whatever the response, it often takes some form of suffering, which doesn't lead to behavior change either. Indeed, these self-denigrating behaviors can actually make things worse. When we are unkind to ourselves, it is hard to be kind to others.

Just as we recommend behaving in compassionate ways to change the relationship with yourself, we also recommend another self-kindness action. Within the suffering just described is often a core sense of being unforgivable for the actions taken while angry. However, your unwillingness to forgive yourself can keep the pain and hurt alive. You might be able to get a sense of this by considering how you feel toward someone who may have harmed you, whom you have not forgiven. As you consider this, we hope you can get a feel for what we mean.

Not forgiving others means that we are harboring old feelings of hurt and holding desires that the harm had not happened, and perhaps even the thought that the other person will "pay" for the harm they did. This experience turned on yourself can have the same qualities. Flexibility and healing are about forgiving. Author and Zen teacher Joko Beck's own Zen teacher put it this way: "Our capacity to know joy is directly related to our capacity to forgive."

The fact that we are inviting you to work on forgiving yourself does not mean we think that aggressive and self-punishing behaviors are acceptable. We recognize that some angry behavior is quite harmful, and it should not be supported or tolerated. However, we also recognize that creating additional harm can never help us recover from these behaviors. Compassion and forgiveness are needed. There is a direct relationship between forgiveness and freedom of the heart. If you have ever felt a kind of freedom of the heart, you will know what we mean. If you have not, then we hope the work in this chapter will help you get there. To begin, let's explore forgiveness more deeply.

Exploring Forgiveness More Deeply

We define forgiveness as an action, not a feeling. As we have explored throughout the book, feelings rise and fall. The feelings that accompany forgiveness can come and go. Behaving in a forgiving way, however, is a choice that is always available to us. You can always choose to treat yourself and others in a forgiving way.

Forgiveness, then, brings together the ACT processes explored in this book: (1) *willingness* to feel what you feel, whether it be shame, sadness, or other feelings; (2) *defusion* from thoughts, such as the ones we've listed concerning self-criticism; (3) *self-as-context*, recognizing that you are more than the experiences you're working on forgiving; (4) *values,* including kindness and perhaps a value of giving itself; and finally (5) *committed action*—treating yourself and others, depending on the forgiveness work, in values-based ways.

Said in another way, forgiveness is about opening up to your emotions, letting go of that protective armor around your heart that might involve hate and criticism, releasing the stories of blame, contacting your vulnerability, and allowing yourself to take the values-based actions needed to heal. This may be a challenging process. Releasing the stories and letting go of the emotions of resentment we harbor toward ourselves isn't easy.

So where do we start? Tara Brach, author of *True Refuge* (2012), tells a story that may be helpful. Imagine a person is walking in the woods and sees a small dog under a tree. As they approach the dog, their initial response is, "Oh, how nice! What a cute dog." As they lean over to pet the dog, it lurches at them, growling and baring its teeth. In this case, the person might shift from being friendly toward the dog to being angry or scared of the dog, even yelling, "Bad dog!" But as they look closer, they discover that the dog's hind leg is caught in a trap. The dog is scared and in pain. Another shift happens. The person says, "Oh my gosh, this poor dog! It needs help."

The person may be wary of getting close enough to risk the chance of being bitten—at least not without the protection of gloves or a blanket. But we want you to notice that their heart has been changed. They see that within this growling, snapping creature is pain. The dog is hurting.

This is the place to start, noticing for yourself what is really going on beneath your own "growling and lurching." You are also hurting and afraid. If you can begin to acknowledge this, you may shift. You may begin to soften your heart concerning your own circumstances.

Unwillingness to forgive often has a narrow, fixed quality. It can seem or feel harsh. It's natural to expect accountability and responsibility for our behaviors, but it is difficult to be responsible when you're too busy blaming, shaming, and criticizing. The suffering goes on. We forget that beneath bluster is pain, yet we keep resisting forgiveness. Let's explore whether there is resistance to forgiveness within you.

Exercise 10.1: Looking at Resistance to Forgiveness

Part I. We invite you to visit a past angry behavior and then reflect on several questions about it.

Start by recalling an event from the distant or recent past when you acted in a harmful way to yourself or someone else as the result of anger. Try to recall an event that is difficult to accept, a time when you really didn't like the way you behaved. Find an event where anger took over, and you either acted on it aggressively or suppressed it to the point of isolation and withdrawal.

After connecting in your memory to this event, ask yourself the following questions:

1. Can I forgive myself for this?

2. What is wrong with forgiving myself for this event?

3. What's wrong with letting go of this self-blame?

As you explore these questions, notice if you find yourself in any way denying the possibility, perhaps stating, *I don't deserve to be forgiven*. Write about what you notice in the space provided.

_____

_____

_____

Part II. Continue reflecting on this event, then respond to another set of questions:

1. In full honesty with myself, what was I afraid of when this event was happening? What fear or hurt was beneath the angry behavior? Beneath the growl and lurch, what was going on?

2. What would it mean to have let those experiences be shown, instead of the anger?

3. Is it possible to shift my heart, allowing myself to contact the vulnerability behind the desire to control?

4. If I'm willing to be vulnerable, would it be possible to let go of self-blame and its ineffective effects?

_____

_____

_____

Notice that we are not asking you to simply forgive. There is a process involved. Along the way, you may encounter emotional difficulties such as grief or guilt. Anthony felt grief when he completed this exercise. He could see how the self-blame kept him in a spiral of shame and anger. He could see that he had not treated himself well and thus had not treated others well either.

For many of us, letting go of the narrative of blame leaves us feeling raw and vulnerable. Showing up to this vulnerability also requires willingness. Now we can see that forgiveness also requires courage. It is a bold action. Sometimes disarming the heart takes both. Let's explore the process of forgiveness further.

The Process of Forgiveness

Forgiveness is not a "one and done" action; it is a process. We might feel forgiving at one time, but think of the event later and again feel bad. This is when it's most important to choose to behave in a forgiving way. You can choose to live a value of kindness a million times as a freely choosing being who is working on the process of self-forgiveness. Defusing from the story line of blame and criticism, connecting to any remorse and its positive message (remorse means you care), and committing to kindness, again and again…and again—that is the process of forgiveness.

In the long run, pursuing forgiveness will help free you from the cycle of hurt, fear, and blame that activates anger. Seeing your leg in the trap and bringing kindness to it will create an experience utterly different from rigidly holding on to stories that trigger the growling and lurching. Again, this will take courage to open up to and accept your own vulnerabilities and be vulnerable with others as well. It will take courage to see which of your own values were violated in either taking an angry action or turning away from your own authenticity by suppressing your experience. And it will take courage to reengage with those very values that were violated. It also means behaving in _truly_ forgiving ways toward yourself and others. False forgiveness is just another strategy to control emotion.

It is also important to practice what we call _taking perspective_. Being able to see situations from multiple points of view is incredibly useful. It can also help you view yourself, taking different perspectives on your own experience. This can assist you in the forgiveness process. Humans have learning histories, some of which are filled with pain. Anger is sometimes the result of these histories.

Being mistreated as a child or having a history of trauma can make you want to control your experiences as an adult. As you work on forgiveness, remember to have compassion for the parts of your history that were painful and perhaps taught you that vulnerability is dangerous. A quick reflection exercise can help.

Exercise 10.2: Practicing Perspective in the Service of Forgiveness

This exercise is designed to help you consider the context of your angry behavior. Remember, taking perspective is designed to help you view what lies beneath the growls and lurches, softening your understanding of yourself. Start by thinking of a time when you were angry and behaved in a way that was inconsistent with your values. You can use the event you selected in exercise 10.1 or select a new event. When you have decided which event to work on, answer the following questions by writing in the space provided.

1. How old were you at the time of the transgression, and how old did you feel? Did you feel younger or older than your actual age? If you felt a different age, explore and explain.

    _____

    _____

    _____

2. What were your intentions? What did you hope for or want when you were angry in this scenario? Dig beneath the surface; what were you really wanting?

    _____

    _____

    _____

3. What were the unintended effects of your angry actions? Notice any vulnerabilities that may have shown up when you realized these unintended effects.

    _____

    _____

    _____

4. What values were hidden or got lost in this struggle? Notice that the values still remain.

_____

_____

_____

5. How might looking at the event from these different perspectives transform this experience into an act of forgiveness?

_____

_____

_____

6. Given what you've just recognized in writing, how might you treat yourself compassionately? If necessary, think back to chapter 9.

_____

_____

_____

Remember, taking perspective on your history, your values, and what you hope to create as you move forward in life will be part of slowly shining a soft, caring light into the darkness, illuminating your path to a kinder and more compassionate existence.

Part of Anthony's forgiveness work was developing compassion for himself and his childhood. He too had been mistreated when he earned poor grades at school. Ironically, he had never wanted to treat any child of his the same way his own father had treated him. He felt shame for not following his values when he acted aggressively toward his son. He blamed himself for transgressing his own commitments. Recognizing and acknowledging his historical context helped him to begin forgiving himself. Anthony realized that part of what he needed to do was take responsibility for his actions and commit to living his values in the present and future.

This leads us to another aspect of forgiveness as a process: it will also involve returning to values-based behavior over and again. "Walk the talk," as the saying goes. Living life from the feet up—not from the head down—is about taking action (even when your mind might object). Putting your feet in motion in the pursuit of values-based living is essential. But keep in mind, we do not fully live our values unless we live them with respect to others and with respect to ourselves. Anthony committed to spending more time with Matthew, helping him to study and achieve better grades. He chose this action to forgive himself, but he also knew he needed to include his value of patience. Anthony worked on modeling patience for his son and, more important, focusing on patience for his own sake. All of these "from the feet up" actions toward Matthew showed his son how much he cared for him.

Finally, it's essential to bring curiosity and interest to the ongoing forgiveness process. By observing your thoughts, feelings, and sensations as you practice forgiving what came before, you'll come to know yourself better and be able to more authentically communicate your experience. Mindful observation of the present moment is the key to freedom. It is the place where choice occurs. And choosing your values can, perhaps, decrease the need to be forgiven over time. In the meantime, let's continue to build the forgiveness as a process muscle with a final forgiveness exercise.

Exercise 10.3: Guided Reflection: Ending the War with Yourself

Often our deepest suffering can come from a sense that something about ourself is fundamentally wrong and unacceptable. Finding a way to make peace with our human imperfections is part of the groundwork for healing. Feel free to close your eyes as you engage in this exercise, reading only as necessary to continue the process. (An audio version of this exercise is available at http://www.newharbinger.com/46530.) Take your time and allow yourself to feel and sense the experience.

Start by finding a comfortable sitting position and take a few moments to gently release the obvious areas of tension in your body. See if you can connect with an intention to open your heart to forgiveness.

Now bring to mind some aspect of yourself that has felt unforgivable due to anger. Perhaps you can't forgive yourself for an angry outburst or hurting others, or for suppressing anger and letting people take advantage of you. Take a moment to fully connect to this aspect of yourself. Notice any aversion you might have toward yourself and this unforgivable behavior.

Now, exploring more deeply, ask yourself:

1. *What needs does this aspect of me have?*

2. *What fears does this aspect want to soothe?*

3. *If this aspect has been harmful to others, were the actions out of hurt and insecurity? Out of the need to feel powerful or safe?*

Look at yourself and your vulnerability through the eyes of the most understanding and loving friend, relative, or higher power.

As you become aware of these underlying wants and fears, allow yourself to feel them directly in your body, heart, and mind. Even though you might dislike the behaviors, try to hold the underlying vulnerability with openness and compassion. Placing your hand on your heart, send a sincere message of self-compassion directly to the places of fear and unmet needs—to the pain that has given rise to what feels unforgivable. You might mentally whisper, *I see how I've caused myself suffering, and I forgive myself now.* Or you might simply offer yourself the words *Forgiven, forgiven.*

Meet whatever arises—fear, judgment, shame, grief—with the message of forgiveness. You can meet your own resistance to forgiving with *Forgiven, forgiven.* You might call to your imagination the presence of someone you consider to be deeply loving and understanding and feel their compassion flowing into you, supporting you. Discover what happens when you bring an unconditionally forgiving heart to the parts of you that are wounded and vulnerable (see Brach, 2012).

When you are done, write any reflections on the experience here:

_____

_____

_____

_____

_____

_____

When you feel unable to forgive yourself, you might believe you don't deserve to be forgiven or fear that if you forgive yourself you'll just do the same thing again. Maybe you're afraid that if you really open yourself to forgiveness, you'll come face to face with some intolerable truth. If these doubts and fears arise, acknowledge and accept them with compassion. Then say to yourself, *It is my intention to forgive myself when I am able.* Your intention to forgive is the seed of forgiveness—this willingness will gradually expand and open your heart.

Forgiveness of Others

In this final section of the chapter, we would like to explore the forgiveness of others. But, before we start, take a moment to notice the nobility of the work possible here. We have all been hurt by others—there is no one exempt from this sort of pain—and we all share a kind of human fallibility based on this simple fact. We are human, and we make human mistakes. We can hurt one another, individually and collectively. Indeed, recognizing this fact holds its own measure of pain. Thus there is dignity and nobility in the act of forgiving others. The Bhagavad Gita counsels, "If you want to see the brave, look to see those who can return love for hatred. If you want to see the heroic, look to those who can forgive."

Does recognizing our common humanity—that we all suffer—make forgiveness of others more possible? Indeed, "If we could read the secret history of our enemies," says Longfellow, "we would find sorrow and suffering enough to disarm all hostility."

So, we ask, can we disarm our hearts in front of others? That doesn't mean we let people hurt us. We can be compassionate and openhearted and still say no. Forgiveness of others does not mean that you condone harmful behavior. It doesn't mean forgive and forget. In fact, you may find it necessary to stand up and prevent harmful behavior. Or it may mean that you may make an inner determination: *I will do all in my power to prevent this suffering from continuing for me or for anyone else.* A common misconception about forgiveness is that it's a weakness or that it ignores harmful behavior. On the contrary, forgiveness can include saying, "I will not let this happen again. I'll do what's necessary."

Forgiveness of others also helps release the world around us from the grip of anger, hatred, hurt, and fear. It allows us to see from—or rest in—the wisdom of kindness. It allows us to move from being in exile to somehow, again, feeling a connection or a trust in this world.

A final and most important question is: Who is the forgiveness for? It is primarily for you. Forgiving another has its own power, for sure, but the greater power lies in what it does for you. It releases you into greater well-being. Forgiveness of others deeply frees your own heart. This is a freedom that we are given no matter what happens outside ourselves. By forgiving others, we can renew ourselves, and we can renew our relationship with the world.

Summary

It is with compassion and forgiveness that we can begin to heal from anger more fully. The six core processes of ACT—acceptance, defusion, present moment, self-as-context, values, and committed action—are the avenues that allow compassion and forgiveness to unfold. Each is a *process*, meaning they entail ongoing work for you to engage in. They are worth every bit of effort you put into them.

With each of these in place, we turn to the last chapter and the utility of anger, exploring its function in places that are potentially healthy and that provide motivation for positive change.

CHAPTER 11

The Beginning and the End Are Intertwined

Nobody can bring you peace but yourself.

—Ralph Waldo Emerson

In this final chapter, we have three main objectives. First, we want to briefly explore the value of anger in the social context, reminding you that anger also serves as a motivating function and can help bring about positive social change. Second, we summarize the story of ACT and what it means to change your relationship with anger. Third, we speak to this chapter's title as you move forward in your journey of managing anger. As with the other chapters, we'll start the first section with true stories of individuals struggling with anger.

The Value of Anger in the Social Context

Anthony is a forty-nine-year-old gay man who has been bullied for his sexual orientation. One incident, among many, occurred while he was simply walking on the sidewalk near his home. A person in a passing car yelled loudly, referencing and degrading his sexual orientation. He described feeling paralyzed at that moment, fearful that he might be physically attacked. In his next therapy session, he described the incident to his therapist. The therapist responded by letting Anthony know that she felt a wave of rising anger toward those who were threatening him. Anthony stated that it was hard for him to feel angry. He mostly felt fear. But as he and his therapist explored social injustice issues and harm against minorities, Anthony began to notice a sense of indignation rising within himself. Together they began to explore how anger might serve an important motivational function concerning social injustice.

Alicia was eight months pregnant and attended, with her partner, one of their final prenatal checkups before the birth. During the appointment, the doctor said, "Please don't forget to take care of your partner. Remember that he has needs." The implication that he was directing her to have sex with her partner caused "a fire" to rise in Alicia's belly. She was baffled by the directive and felt instantly angry at this insensitive patriarchal remark. She managed to respond "What?" in a stern tone. The doctor responded, "I understand that you are feeling emotional." Alicia was stunned and said no more. Alicia reported in her therapy session that she felt shame for not addressing the doctor and his behavior at that moment.

Anger Is Not Always Our Enemy

It makes sense that both Anthony and Alicia felt anger in response to these encounters. The Dalai Lama tells us that we *should* be angered by suffering, that it should stir in us the kind of compassion that moves us to take action in the face of injustice and discrimination. It can move us to stop oppression. Anger in response to social injustice—whether it be based on sexual orientation, gender, race, religion, economic status, age, or disability—is normal. When we are moved to anger by our own or someone else's suffering, we can also be moved, literally. Anger can call us to action to create a more just or equal society.

So even though we explored compassion and forgiveness in the prior two chapters, we also want to recognize the value of anger in making a healthy change. Indeed, just because we call for compassion and forgiveness doesn't mean that we wouldn't also call for anger, especially in the service of prosocial and caring behavior. The context and cause of the anger matters a great deal. Authentically reflecting on what led to your experience of anger, as we have been working on here, will help you know.

The social issues that might elicit anger are legion. The issue deserves a book of its own. Rather than cover each potential category, we'll simply describe the broader issue and then explore an example to get you thinking more about anger and social issues.

Anger in Social Contexts

If we think of emotions in evolutionary terms, we might see how they help us be sensitive to environmental cues relevant to our survival. Anger in the face of a threat makes sense. It can fuel us to move, protecting ourselves and others from danger. Social injustice can be viewed as one such threat, and anger is the prototypical protest emotion.

One way to harness anger and outrage is to view it as information. Anger helps us notice that boundaries have been crossed. Exploring what the anger is trying to communicate can help you identify social problems and confront them—through conversation, protest, or advocacy. Anger also has an alerting function. It tells others that it's important to listen to our words and pay attention to our actions.

Anger is often posited as the necessary catalyzing force to engender change. While anger can be painful and sometimes volatile, it can also be instrumental. When we channel it wisely, we can use anger to spur meaningful action, advocate for ourselves and others, and affect change. Let's look closer.

ANGER AND SOCIAL JUSTICE

Anger has traditionally been associated with aggression and antagonistic behavior in social contexts. However, a series of studies (Van Doorn, Zeelenberg, Breugelmans, Berger, & Okimoto, 2018) revealed that experiences of third-party anger (anger experienced when observing that harm is being done to someone) can also lead to prosocial behavior. Specifically, there is some evidence that anger can promote positive behaviors such as social sharing, compensation to a victim, and help for the disadvantaged. Anger can tune people in to concerns about equity and the need for reparation.

Other research has shown that moral outrage was a stronger predictor for prosocial behavior than sympathy (Eisenberg & Fabes, 1990). Anger can be a deeply moral emotion aimed at maintaining moral order and restoring social order when ruptured. Indeed, anger can be one reason that social justice movements begin.

Exercise 11.1: Assessing Your Anger in Social Contexts

Recall a time when you witnessed or experienced a social injustice. This can be anything that includes oppression, inequality, or social injustice of underprivileged groups. As you recall the situation, notice if you experience any anger in response to what was happening. We understand that these situations are complex and can be difficult to tease out in any single exercise. If it is easier, you can simply get in touch with any anger you have experienced in response to others suffering harm. Write about the experience and your feeling of anger in response to collective suffering.

_____

_____

_____

_____

_____

_____

If you have experienced anger in response to these kinds of situations, respond to these questions:

1. Is there a way for you to transform the anger into values-based action? How can anger be your ally?

    _____

    _____

    _____

2. As you experience the anger, is there a call for you to do something larger than you have done before?

    _____

    _____

    _____

The point of this exercise isn't to tell you that you must go out and do something prosocial. Rather, it is for you to see the usefulness of anger, given the right context. If you are motivated to make a change based on this emotion, then anger has served its positive purpose.

When a moral order is ruptured or violated, anger can serve as a signal identifying and communicating the magnitude of the violation. It is also a source of energy aimed at restoring and repairing the violation. Anger is a normal and necessary response to oppressive acts, especially when facing pervasive injustices such as racial and gender discrimination. Learning to relate to and channel our anger can make us more effective advocates and activists. In this larger context of humankind, you may be motivated by anger to take action.

Let's return to Anthony and Alicia as individual examples of prosocial change. Anthony harnessed his anger by helping the LGBTQ+ community. He used the anger to motivate himself to engage in something he found profoundly valuable. His anger was transformed into energy, giving him what he needed to help other sexual minorities in need. Alicia channeled her anger in two different ways. First, after "finding her words," she confronted her doctor. She let him know that what he had done was not okay, and she asked for respect in the future. Second, she started a small local group for women with children. The group focused on supporting each other and finding ways to effectively communicate about equality and sensitivity to women's issues during pregnancy and birth. They wrote letters to obstetrics clinics around the nation. Both Anthony and Alicia used their anger to help them make a change.

Finally, when considering any potential prosocial action, we urge you to do a little homework first. Just as anger can give you information identifying and communicating the magnitude of the violation, practical information can help you understand the context of the work you hope to do. Let's take a look at anger and gender as an example. You may be surprised by what you learn.

LEARNING ABOUT ANGER AND GENDER

Let's first quickly dispel any misinformation that you might have been given about how men and women experience anger. For instance, you might believe that men experience anger more than women. Two researchers, DiGiuseppe and Trafrate (2004), found that men and women experience feelings of anger about equally. Both men and women experience the same intensity of anger, and each gender seeks treatment and anger management programs about equally. The researchers note that differences between men and women emerge in the expression of anger. Men tend to express anger with more aggression, passive-aggression, and coercion than do women. They also tend to deal with their anger impulsively and more commonly have a revenge motive when engaging in angry behavior.

Additionally, aggressive behavior in men tends to stretch across cultures and time (Pinker, 2011). Conversely, women tend to hang on to anger longer and are less likely to express anger outwardly but more likely to talk about their anger. They also tend to be more resentful when feeling anger. Finally, both men and women become less angry as they age, with anger decreasing after age fifty. However, men still have a greater tendency to be aggressive while angry, and women tend to have longer anger episodes (DiGiuseppe & Tafrate, 2003).

It is important to recognize that men and women are socialized to express anger differently. This may be a large part of why researchers see these differences—and perhaps why some stereotypes of men and women's anger persist. Even from a young age, angry expressions in girls is viewed as "unladylike" (even to this day), and anger expressed aggressively in boys is considered to be more "manly." In this way, it is more socially acceptable for men to express anger than for women. The unfortunate fallout is that it may seem that women do not get angry, when clearly they do. But girls' emotions are policed from childhood. And anger remains the least acceptable emotion for girls and women, potentially because it is the first defense against injustice. The critical thing to remember is that neither men nor women own anger. It is a human emotion and doesn't "belong" to either gender.

Did any of this surprise you? If so, then all the more reason to gather information when taking action in the service of prosocial behavior. Dispelling myths and stereotypes will give you a leg up as you embark on any of these endeavors.

Exercise 11.2: Channeling Your Anger for Good

Let's explore the situation from exercise 11.1 again. Again, recall the social injustice wherein you noticed anger. Notice what the anger "hopes" for, what you are wanting to change.

1.   What does anger communicate to you? What does it tell you about what you value?

2.   Is the anger linked to something good for the whole community?

3.   What are the ultimate benefits of the actions taken, even if motivated by anger?

Write your responses here:

_____

_____

_____

_____

_____

We would argue that a world without anger could be a compliant and quiescent world, but likely not a just world. Anger can be a positive force in society. It can help create and maintain a moral order or restore social order.

ACT and Changing Your Relationship with Anger

Throughout this book, we have explored different ways to help you be more flexible with the emotion of anger, committing to what you care about most as an alternative to acting out or suppressing this emotion. As you choose to be willing to feel anger and the emotions that lie beneath it, such as vulnerability, and as you defuse from angry and critical thoughts, you will find a kind of openness to your experience that will give you freedom. As you turn your attention to the present moment, being more aware of the here and now instead of overly focusing on the past or future, joy will become more available and your sensing of the world more alive. As you connect to a sense of yourself that is more than your emotions and more than your anger, you will open to the vast number of experiences that flow through you and are there to have as you taste life. And finally, as you choose to live your values through committed action, your meaning in life will unfold, your purpose revealed.

We hope that this flexible stance of being open, aware, and engaged will move you to a wise relationship with yourself and others—living a connected and loving life.

Ending the Book But Starting the Journey

A key issue that we have worked on in this book is how to be flexible in your relationship with yourself and your emotions and thoughts. We have worked on how to move assertively in the direction that honors what you care most about. We have now reached the end of this singular path: the one defined by the pages of this book. However, the journey goes on. The end and the beginning are intertwined. Your work will continue to unfold as you take with you the experiences of completing this book—to be applied to your everyday life—and the desire to no longer be a slave to anger. Indeed, there may even be times when anger is your ally, serving you in social justice issues.

May the freedom you have found in letting go of trying to control your emotions and others' be fully available to you as you live an unfolding life guided by your values.

References

Brach, T. (2012). *True refuge: Finding peace and freedom in your own awakened heart.* New York: Bantam.

DiGiuseppe, R., & Tafrate, R. C. (2003). Anger treatment for adults: A meta-analytic review. *Clinical Psychology: Science and Practice, 10,* 70–84. https://doi.org/10.1093/clipsy/10.1.70

Doran, G. T. (1981). There's a SMART way to write management's goals and objectives. *Management Review, 70,* 35–36.

Eisenberg, N., & Fabes, R. A. (1990). Empathy: Conceptualization, measurement, and relation to prosocial behavior. *Motivation and Emotion, 14,* 131–149. https://doi.org/10.1007/BF00991640

Hayes, S. C., Strosahl, K. D., & Wilson, K. G. (2012). *Acceptance and commitment therapy: The process and practice of mindful change* (2nd ed.). New York: Guilford Press.

Lee, A. H., & DiGiuseppe, R. (2018). Anger and aggression treatments: A review of meta-analyses. *Current Opinion in Psychology, 19,* 65–74. https://doi.org/10.1016/j.copsyc.2017.04.004

Pinker, S. (2011). *The better angels of our nature: Why violence has declined.* New York: Viking.

Stemmler, G., Aue, T., & Wacker, J. (2007). Anger and fear: Separable effects of emotion and motivational direction on somatovisceral responses. *International Journal of Psychophysiology, 66,* 141–153.

Van Doorn, J., Zeelenberg, M., Breugelmans, S. M., Berger, S., & Okimoto, T. G. (2018). Prosocial consequences of third-party anger. *Theory and Decision, 84,* 585–599.

Robyn D. Walser, PhD, is director of TL Consultation and Psychological Services, and codirector of Bay Area Trauma Recovery Clinical Services. She works at the National Center for PTSD, developing and disseminating innovative ways to translate science into practice; and serves as assistant clinical professor in the department of psychology at the University of California, Berkeley. As a licensed clinical psychologist, she maintains an international training, consulting, and therapy practice. Walser has authored and coauthored six books: *The Heart of ACT, Learning ACT, The Mindful Couple, Acceptance and Commitment Therapy for the Treatment of Post-Traumatic Stress Disorder and Trauma-Related Problems*, and *ACT for Clergy and Pastoral Counselors*.

Manuela O'Connell is an acceptance and commitment therapy (ACT) therapist and trainer who conducts workshops and seminars in English and Spanish. She is professor at Universidad Favaloro at Buenos Aires, Argentina, and holds ACT and mindfulness workshops for the general public. She has written a self-help book in Spanish titled *Una vida valiosa*, and was a contributor to *The Heart of ACT*.

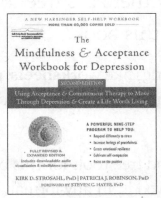
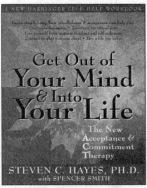
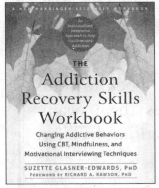

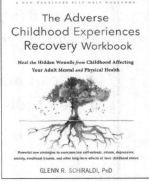

Did you know there are free tools you can download for this book?

Free tools are things like **worksheets, guided meditation exercises**, and **more** that will help you get the most out of your book.

You can download free tools for this book—whether you bought or borrowed it, in any format, from any source—from the **New Harbinger** website. All you need is a NewHarbinger.com account. Just use the URL provided in this book to view the free tools that are available for it. Then, click on the "download" button for the free tool you want, and follow the prompts that appear to log in to your NewHarbinger.com account and download the material.

You can also save the free tools for this book to your **Free Tools Library** so you can access them again anytime, just by logging in to your account! Just look for this button on the book's free tools page:

+ save this to my
free tools library

If you need help accessing or downloading free tools, visit **newharbinger.com/faq** or contact us at customerservice@newharbinger.com.

CELEBRATING
40 YEARS